Dawson
29/5/97
£17.95

SOU

Nature and Nurture
An Introduction to
Human Behavioral Genetics

About the Author

Robert Plomin (Ph.D., University of Texas at Austin) first became interested in genetics at the early age or 10, when he brought a book on evolution to school for show-and-tell. Astonished by the power and simplicity of evolution and the key role played by heredity, he was anxious to share his "find" with his elementary school class. But instead of the anticipated excitement of his classmates, he found himself whisked out of class to the principal's office and sent home until his parents could come to the school for a conference. It was then considered a mortal sin to believe in evolution and Plomin's school was Catholic. Far from purging him of thoughts of evolution, however, this event convinced him of the importance of these ideas and, perhaps because they were forbidden, made them all the more enticing.

More interested in psychology than biology, in the late 1960s Plomin began graduate school in psychology at the University of Texas at Austin, which also happened to be one of two or three places in the world at that time that had a program in behavioral genetics.

Robert Plomin is currently co-director of the Center for Developmental and Health Genetics and Professor in the Department of Human Development and Family Studies at the Pennsylvania State University.

Currently President of the Behavior Genetics Association, Plomin is the author of numerous books and articles in the field of behavioral genetics, including *Development, Genetics, and Psychology* (Erlbaum, 1986) and *Nature and Nurture During Infancy and Childhood* (co-authored with J. C. DeFries and D. W. Fulker, Cambridge University Press, 1988.)

Nature and Nurture
An Introduction to
Human Behavioral Genetics

Robert Plomin

The Pennsylvania State University

Brooks/Cole Publishing Company
Pacific Grove, California

I(T)P™ The trademark ITP is used under license.

Brooks/Cole Publishing Company
A Division of Wadsworth, Inc.
© 1990 by Wadsworth, Inc., Belmont, California 94002.

Printed in the United States of America
10 9 8 7 6 5 4

Library of Congress Cataloging in Publication Data
Plomin, Robert [date]
    Nature and nurture: an introduction to human behavioral genetics
 / Robert Plomin.
      p.   cm.
    Bibliography: p.
    Includes index.
    ISBN 0-534-10768-0
    1. Behavior genetics. 2. Human genetics. 3. Human behavior.
    4. Nature and nurture.   I. Title.
    QH457.P57 1989
155.42'2—dc20   89-9725
                                        CIP

Now O/P- 28/1/4

Sponsoring Editor: *Vicki Knight*
Editorial Assistant: *Heather Reidl*
Production Editor: *Linda Loba*
Manuscript Editor: *Evelyn Ward*
Permissions Editor: *Carline Haga*
Interior Design: *Katherine Minerva*
Cover Design: *Kathryn B. Stark*
Cover Photo: *Tony Salazar Photography*
Art Coordinator: *Sue C. Howard*
Photo Editor and Researcher: *Sue C. Howard*
Typesetting: *Bookends Typesetting*
Printing and Binding: *Malloy Lithographing, Inc.*

Preface

As behavioral genetics has become more accepted during the past decade, I frequently have been asked if there is a brief introduction to the field. The answer is no—there really is no introduction other than entire textbooks. The purpose of this book is to fill that gap—to provide a brief and accessible overview of the methods and findings of behavioral genetics.

The book includes five chapters. The first introduces the substance of behavioral genetics by asking why people differ. Chapter 2 discusses how heredity affects behavior. This chapter introduces molecular genetics and Mendelian genetics in so far as these topics apply to an understanding of behavioral genetics. The third chapter presents the methods of behavioral genetics that permit us to explore the effects of heredity on behavior. An overview of the evidence for genetic influence in such domains as intelligence, personality, and psychopathology is included in Chapter 4. The final chapter considers the nurture side of nature-nurture as viewed from the perspective of behavioral genetics.

My motivation for writing this book is to give behavioral genetics "away," so that it can be understood and used by people who are not behavioral geneticists. That is, I believe that the best behavioral genetics research of the future will not be conducted by behavioral geneticists. It will be done by researchers in other fields who use this approach to answer theory-driven questions that arise in their fields. For this reason, it is important that social and behavioral scientists of the future know about behavioral genetics.

I'd like to express my appreciation to the following reviewers for their suggestions: Professor Thomas Bouchard, University of Minnesota; Professor Steven Gangestad, University of New Mexico; Dr. R. Sergio Guglielmi, University of Virginia; Professor Kathleen McCartney, University of New Hampshire; Professor Daniel Ozer, Boston University; Professor Sandra Scarr, University of Virginia; and Dr. Nancy Segal, University of Minnesota.

Robert Plomin

Contents

Chapter 5
How Are Nurture and Nature Important?
115

1

Why
Are People
Different?

Why *are* people different? Why are some people heavier, why are some smarter, why are some more depressed? For thousands of years, two broad categories of answers have been given to the question of the origins of individual differences: heredity (nature) and environment (nurture). This is the fundamental question of behavioral genetics. Research on nature and nurture is one of the oldest and most controversial areas in the social and behavioral sciences, going back well over one hundred years to Francis Galton in England. A half cousin of Charles Darwin, Galton's life as an inventor and explorer changed as he read Darwin's famous book on evolution. Galton understood that evolution depends on heredity, and in the last two decades of his life, he began to ask whether heredity affects human behavior. He suggested the major methods of human behavioral genetics—family, twin, and adoption designs—and conducted the first systematic family studies that showed that behavioral traits "run in families." Galton also invented correlation, one of the fundamental concepts of statistics, in order to describe resemblance among family members.

Although Galton is the father of human behavioral genetics, his role in the history of the behavioral sciences is often neglected. In part, this neglect is due to his interest in individual differences. Galton's interest was out of step with the early history of psychology, which focused on species-wide principles of behavior. At nearly the same time that the field of psychology was beginning with the study of general principles of human perception, Galton was studying individual differences in people's perceptions and reaction times.

A few twin and adoption studies were conducted during the 1920s and 1930s, but these had little impact on the social and behavioral sciences. Studies of animals had a greater effect in demonstrating the importance of genetic influence, perhaps because examining the role of genetic influence on nonhuman behavior was not as troubling. For example, a famous artificial selection study showed that it is possible to breed one line of rats for their ability to learn to run through a maze quickly with few errors and to breed another line that was extremely poor in maze performance. Another type of animal study compared behavioral traits for inbred strains of mice. Inbred strains are created by inbreeding through brother-sister matings for twenty generations. This inbreeding produces a strain in which all mice are virtually identical genetically to other members of the strain. There are over a hundred such inbred strains. Behavioral differences that exist between such inbred strains can be attributed to their genetic differences. Behavioral studies of inbred strains in the 1950s uncovered evidence for genetic influence. In large part, this work led to the first behavioral genetics textbook in 1960 by John Fuller and W. Robert Thompson.

The human behavioral genetic research that had been begun in the 1920s with twin and adoption studies continued into the 1960s but remained outside the mainstream of the social and behavioral sciences. However, the success of animal research in behavioral genetics stimulated increasing interest in the possibility of genetic influence on human behavior. In 1963 an influential article reviewed family, twin, and adoption data for IQ scores and concluded that genetic influence is important for this trait (Erlenmeyer-Kimling & Jarvik, 1963). In 1966 the adoption study of schizophrenia by Leonard Heston, mentioned previously in the preface, was critically important in suggesting the influence of heredity in psychopathology. These and other studies began to build some slight momentum for research on human behavioral genetics. However, this momentum came to a halt in 1969 when Arthur Jensen published a paper that reviewed the evidence for genetic influence on IQ scores and suggested that the average IQ difference between blacks and whites may in part be due to genetic differences. Jensen's article provoked a furious response unparalleled in the social and behavioral sciences. The reaction threatened the existence of the fledgling field of human behavioral genetics, even though very few behavioral geneticists studied racial differences. The furor subsided only gradually during the following decade as the spotlight moved from racial differences to new information about genetic influence on individual differences in cognitive abilities, psychopathology, and personality.

During the 1980s, a remarkable turnaround occurred in which antipathy toward human behavioral genetics turned into acceptance. For example, a 1987 survey of over one thousand social and behavioral scientists and educators indicated that most had accepted a significant role for heredity on IQ scores, traditionally one of the most controversial areas in behavioral genetics (Synderman & Rothman, 1987). Although the reasons for this dramatic shift toward acceptance of behavioral genetics research have not been systematically examined, the change was caused in part by the compelling convergence of results that point to influence of heredity on human behavior. These results are described in Chapter 4.

Individual and Group Differences

A fundamental point about behavioral genetics is that it focuses on specific differences among individuals rather than average differences between groups of people. Behavioral genetics is the study of genetic and environmental factors that create behavioral differences among individuals. Heredity refers to the transmission of these differences from parent to offspring. For example, height is highly heritable. This means that differences due to heredity play a role in the differences in height from one person to another. Behavioral genetics is not equipped to address the causes of the average height of the human species, or the fact that on average the human species is getting taller, or the causes of the average difference in height between males and females. These are average group differences. The distinction between individual differences and average group differences is critical, because behavioral genetics focuses on the genetic and environmental sources of individual behavioral differences but has little to say about the causes of differences between groups. For instance, behavioral genetics can tell why some children are delayed in their use of language but it cannot tell us why the human species as a whole used language or why girls on average tend to perform better than boys on verbal tests.

There are three reasons why geneticists are interested in individual behavioral differences. First, individual differences are substantial. For example, individuals differ considerably in scores on vocabulary tests—on a moderately difficult test, the top scorers will get five times as many words correct as low scorers (Plomin & DeFries, 1985). A related point is that differences among individuals are far greater than average differences between groups. Although girls on average perform better than boys on tests of verbal ability, this statistically significant difference is small. That is, if all you know is whether a child is a boy or a girl, you know very little about that child's verbal ability, because the individual differences between boys and girls can be great.

Another reason we are interested in differences among individuals is that issues relevant to society often involve individual differences. For example, although it is interesting to ask why the human species uses language, more relevant to society are questions such as why some children are slow in learning to use language, why some are delayed in reading skills, and why some people are more verbally fluent than others. A third reason is that the causes of individual differences are not necessarily related to the causes of average differences between groups. For instance, the causes of individual differences in tests of verbal ability could be substantially influenced by genetic factors. However, the average difference between girls and boys on these tests could be environmental

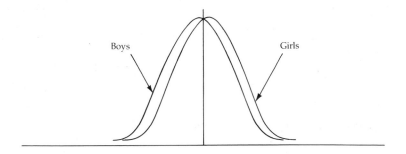

Figure 1.1. Distribution of vocabulary scores
for boys and girls. Although girls outperform boys, the overlap
in the two distributions exceeds 90 percent.

in origin. Although the difference between boys and girls might be biological, such as hormonal differences, it is possible that nurture rather than nature is responsible for the difference—perhaps mothers talk to their daughters more than to their sons.

Thinking about Heredity

One of the best ways to begin looking at behavior from the behavioral genetics perspective is to think of individual differences that interest you personally, preferably a behavioral characteristic for which you are at the high or low extreme. Perhaps you are musically gifted, especially adept at learning languages, or good at sports. If you are neither above or below average on such abilities, then consider personality traits such as activity level, emotionality, or shyness. When you think about "your" trait, one of the first questions that will come to mind is the why question. Why, for example, do people differ so much in athletic ability? It is easy to think of possible environmental explanations—your parents might have pushed you into sports, special training programs or equipment may have been available, or there may have been some role model that captured your imagination at an early age. However, it is possible that you may have inherited athletic ability from your parents. Of course, it takes practice to be an athlete, but you practiced because you were good at it. The goal of this book is to convince you that it is reasonable to expect that some of the behavioral differences among people are genetic in origin. The goal is *not* to say that every difference is genetic in origin—in fact, a major theme of this book is that behavioral genetic research demonstrates that environmental influences are also important.

Thinking about Environment

You probably do not need to be convinced that environment can make people different. Many people feel that environmental influences are the most reasonable explanation of individual differences. At least four factors contribute to this belief. First, in America, our founding fathers wrote that all people are created equal, and it seems to follow that differences among people must be due to differences in experience. This interpretation is literally wrong. Our founding fathers were not so naive as to think that all men are created *identical;* the point of a democracy is that all people should be treated equally despite their differences.

Second, behaviorism reigned for nearly 50 years, up to the past decade, as a dominant explanation of differences. Behaviorism focuses on environmental stimuli that change behavior—stimulus and response. From the start, behaviorism denied any role for hereditary differences. In his book *Behaviorism,* published in 1925, John B. Watson concluded "that there is no such thing as an inheritance of capacity, talent, temperament, mental constitution and characteristics. These things again depend on training that goes on mainly in the cradle" (pp. 74–75). Although Watson recognized hereditary influence on physical traits, he denied any influence of heredity on behavioral traits and said that given sufficient environmental control, he could train any healthy baby to become a doctor, artist, or thief, regardless of the child's heredity. Few would accept Watson's dictum today; nonetheless, his emphasis on nurture rather than nature continues to affect the social and behavioral sciences.

Third, environmental explanations of behavior fit with our own day-to-day experiences in how we learn to adapt to our environment. For example, if you are shy, it is not difficult to think back to experiences to which you can attribute the source of your shyness. Heredity, on the other hand, cannot be experienced in this immediate and intimate way.

For the very reason that it is so easy to explain anything environmentally, one should be cautious about environmental explanations. One example I have witnessed on several occasions involves parents' attempts to explain the shyness of their children. Answers are typically of two types: "My child is shy because we did not take her out to visit other people enough when she was young," or "My child is shy because we took her out too much when she was young." Among behavioral geneticists, there is a saying that parents are environmentalists until they have more than one child. With one child, it seems possible to explain anything that happens. However, when their second child turns out to be different in many ways from the first child, parents realize that they did not treat the two children differently enough to account for the behavioral differences that are so apparent between them. With their second child, parents become more accepting of the possibility of hereditary differences. (You might, at this point, find yourself wondering why there should be differences within a family if genetics are so important. First-degree relatives, however, are only 50 percent similar genetically, which means that they are also 50 percent different genetically. This is discussed in Chapter 3.)

Fourth, environmental explanations seem reasonable because we generally feel that environment can be changed but that we are stuck with our heredity. However, thinking that nothing can be done to alter genetic effects comes from misunderstanding how genes work. Genetic effects do not take away free will; they do not determine behavior. Genetic influences are just that—influences, tendencies, propensities. How genes work is the topic of Chapter 2.

The Challenge

A major challenge for the field of behavioral genetics lies in the fact that answers to why individuals differ on many behavioral traits are not yet known. The examples mentioned previously—musical ability, language learning ability, athletic ability—have not yet been studied sufficiently to enable us to draw any conclusions about the contribution of heredity. Many important facets of behavior have yet to be considered from the perspective of behavioral genetics. Moreover, our intuition about which traits should and should not reflect genetic influence is of little use. For example, students usually think that biological traits will show greater genetic influence than will behavioral traits. In fact, some biological traits—such as proneness to the major types of cancer and allergies—show little inherited genetic influence. In general, behavioral traits seem to show as much genetic influence as do most biological traits. Consider personality traits. Intuition may tell us that a trait such as activity level is more likely to be heritable than a trait such as shyness, because activity level seems somehow more closely linked to biology than does shyness. However, behavioral genetic studies indicate that shyness shows as much if not more genetic influence throughout the life course as other personality traits. What is needed is investigation, not intuition. My hope for this book is that it will spark sufficient interest in behavioral genetics that some students will join this effort to answer the question of why people differ.

2

How Do Genes Influence Behavior?

How does heredity affect behavior? How can the simple chemical codes of DNA (deoxyribose nucleic acid) contained in each cell of our body relate to the complexity of the behavior of the whole organism? In other words, how do genes influence behavior?

Very little molecular genetics (the biochemistry of DNA) needs to be learned for one to understand the basics of behavioral genetics. This is because behavioral genetic methods derive from laws of hereditary transmission. Although molecular genetics keeps up a steady outpouring of fascinating findings concerning the workings of DNA, nothing in molecular genetics has changed the basic laws of hereditary transmission discovered by Gregor Mendel, a monk who studied heredity in pea plants over a hundred years ago. Nonetheless, it is useful to describe enough of the workings of DNA to dispel mystical notions that students often have about the relationship between genes and behavior. For example, students often wrongly assume that genes somehow encode behavior directly —that DNA is a master puppeteer within us, pulling our strings as needed. The purpose of this chapter is to provide necessary information about DNA and its functions in order to help you understand what it means to say that genes influence behavior.

DNA

Genes are stretches of DNA, the helix-shaped double coils in the nucleus of each of our trillions of cells. The double-coiled DNA constitute the core of the 23 pairs of human chromosomes (or "colored bodies," referring to chromosomes' tendency to absorb certain stains), collections of thousands of genes. Although we can see chromosomes under the microscope, the DNA molecule itself is so tiny that it cannot be viewed even with an electron microscope. DNA is like a spiral staircase; each step in the staircase is one combination of four ring-shaped carbon-nitrogen molecules called nucleotide bases: adenine, thymine, guanine, and cytosine. As shown in Figure 2.1, these four bases can occur in any sequence along the backbone of single-stranded DNA. However, the complementary strand (the other side of the spiral staircase) is limited, because adenine can bond only with thymine and guanine can bond only with cytosine. Thus, as shown in Figure 2.1, the possible sequences involve A paired with T, T with A, G with C, or C with G. If the sequence of one strand of DNA is known, the sequence of the complementary strand is also known. This complementary structure permits accurate duplication of each DNA strand during the growth process.

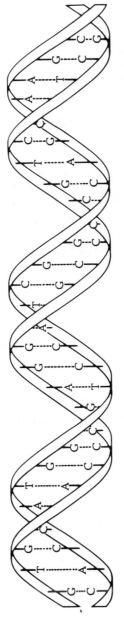

Figure 2.1. The nucleotide basis of DNA.

This simple structure of DNA contains specific instructions honed by evolution for the development of the millions of species we see around us. Even the tiniest life forms, viruses, which take over the genetic machinery of the cells of host organisms, have dozens of genes involving about 50,000 base pairs of DNA. The simplest, complete, single-celled organisms such as bacteria contain one chromosome with millions of nucleotide base pairs of DNA. Human beings have 23 pairs of chromosomes. The average chromosome contains about 80 million base pairs, a total of 3.5 billion base pairs in the nucleus of each of our trillions of cells. DNA has two basic functions: translation and transmission.

Translation

Translation refers to the process by which DNA codes for the production of proteins responsible for most of what we are. Proteins coded by DNA form the structure of cells, the connective tissue between cells, and muscles. These proteins also perform physiological functions; for example, neurotransmitters and hormones are proteins. In addition, there are specialized proteins (enzymes) that determine which chemical reactions occur in a particular cell. Proteins consist of chains of specific sequences of amino acids from 50 to 2000 amino acids in length. The complexity of the situation is apparent when one realizes that most cells have over 2000 varieties of proteins.

By 1953 the central "dogma" of molecular genetics was understood: DNA is transcribed by an intermediate molecule, messenger RNA, which travels outside the nucleus to ribosomes situated in the cell body, where the genetic message— including messages that code for proteins that affect behavior— is translated into sequences of amino acids (see Figure 2.2). The code for DNA involves three steps in the spiral staircase: each amino acid in each protein is coded by a sequence of three nucleotide base pairs of DNA. The triplet code was fully

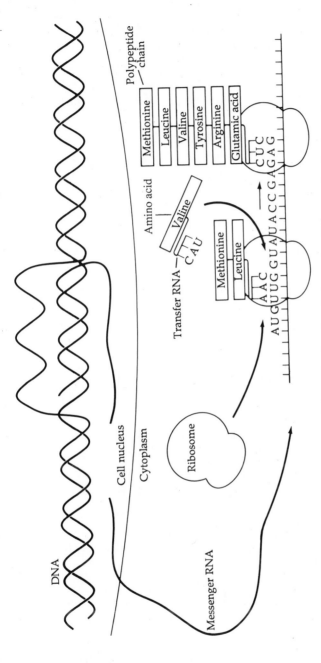

Figure 2.2. The "central dogma" of molecular genetics. The genetic message of DNA is transcribed to messenger RNA except that T (thymine) bases are replaced with the closely related U (uracil) base. The messenger RNA travels outside the nucleus to ribosomes in the cell body. Transfer RNA transports the 20 amino acids to the ribosomes, where amino acids are added one by one to the growing chain of amino acids. Each of the 20 amino acids that comprise proteins is specified by a "codon" made up of three sequential RNA bases. (Adapted from "The mechanism of evolution" by F. J. Ayala. *Scientific American,* 239:56–69. Copyright 1978 by Scientific American, Inc. All rights reserved.)

15

deciphered by 1966 for the 20 amino acids and DNA "punctuation," which includes start and stop signals. This genetic code is the same for essentially all living organisms, including plants, insects, and human beings. The average protein involves a unique sequence of about 400 amino acids and thus requires 1200 nucleotide DNA base pairs for its coding. However, such "structural" genes that code amino acid sequences of proteins comprise only a small fraction of DNA. Another important product of transcribed DNA are amino acid sequences that regulate the transcription of other bits of DNA.

In the early 1970s, just when most people thought that molecular miracles were over, recombinant DNA techniques were discovered and led to another heady round of advances that continues today. Recombinant DNA techniques make it possible to recombine DNA from any organism with bacterial DNA in order to study the function of DNA of higher organisms translated in the simple bacterial cell. The critical step was the discovery of restriction enzymes that cut DNA at specific sites and create "sticky" ends. By cutting both human DNA and bacterial DNA with the same restriction enzyme, the sticky ends of a human DNA fragment can be inserted within the sticky ends of bacterial DNA. The first recombinant DNA was formed in 1973. It was quickly realized that recombinant DNA techniques made it possible for the first time to analyze DNA of higher organisms by inserting fragments of DNA into bacteria. If a specific gene can be inserted, the bacteria will then transcribe this gene and produce the protein for which it codes. In this way, bacteria have, for example, been turned into factories for the production of two human proteins, growth hormone and insulin.

Recombinant DNA techniques have also been useful in obtaining genetic markers that make it possible to map genes to chromosomes. When human DNA is cut with a particular restriction enzyme that recognizes a specific sequence of six nucleotide bases, DNA of an individual who does not have one of these bases will not be cut at that particular site. Thus, instead of having two shorter fragments of DNA, such an individual will have one longer fragment. This DNA variation is called a restriction fragment length polymorphism (RFLP, pronounced "riff-lip"). Over a thousand RFLPs that vary among human beings have been discovered. RFLPs close together on chromosomes can be detected, and in this way, RFLP maps of chromosomes have been constructed. A human "gene map" of this type was announced in 1987. Such a gene map is valuable because disorders caused by a single gene can be linked to one of these markers. This linkage indicates the chromosomal location of the gene. The gene itself can be taken out and inserted into bacteria; the resulting gene product can be studied to determine how the gene causes the disorder.

Although recombinant DNA is an extremely important development, its relevance for behavioral genetics lies in the future. By the turn of the century, it may be possible to obtain a gene map of each individual so that we can begin to compare DNA variation among individuals directly rather than resorting to the indirect methods of behavioral genetics described in the next chapter.

Transmission

In review, the first function of DNA is to code and regulate protein production. In this way, differences in DNA of individuals are translated into protein differences, some of which can contribute to behavioral differences among individuals. The second function of DNA is equally important for behavioral genetics. DNA must replicate itself faithfully, including replication in the cells called gametes (sperm and egg), so that hereditary transmission occurs. The gametes are specialized cells that through a process called meiosis have only one member of each pair of chromosomes. Thus when sperm fertilize an egg, the resulting zygote has a full complement of 23 pairs of chromosomes. The fidelity of DNA replication is amazing, with an error occuring perhaps only once in a billion replications. These errors are called mutations and are the ultimate cause of genetic variability.

Mendel's experiments with pea plants during the mid-nineteenth century led him to deduce the laws of hereditary transmission. He discovered that there are two hereditary elements, one from the mother and one from the father. We now call these hereditary elements alleles, which are alternate forms of genes on each matched pair of chromosomes. *Locus* is the word used to refer to the place on a chromosome where alleles reside. (The word *gene* can be confusing because it is used to refer both to allele and locus.) For example, the ABO blood group refers to a locus near the tip of chromosome 9, where any pairing of three alleles can be found, A, B, or O.

The main point of Mendel's work was the discovery that alleles do not blend in inheritance, as was commonly believed at the time. Mendel showed that instead of blending, alleles have discrete effects that can reappear in later generations. He also showed that some alleles are dominant and others are recessive. For a recessive allele to show up, a person would have to have the recessive allele at that locus on both chromosomes. For example, phenylketonuria (PKU), which causes mental retardation if untreated, is a recessive, single-gene disease. A person who has only one recessive allele for a particular disorder is called a carrier because he carries one allele for PKU but will not show the disease. However, a carrier can pass on the PKU allele to his offspring, who would show the disease if the other parent was also a carrier and transmitted the recessive allele to the offspring. Carriers do not show the disease because their other allele is able to produce enough of the enzyme needed to metabolize phenylalanine sufficiently so that brain damage is avoided during early development. However, many other alleles do not operate in a simple dominant-recessive manner. As discussed later, behavioral traits appear to be affected by genes that generally operate in an additive manner. That is, alleles at many loci are additive in their effect on the trait. For example, genetic influence on intelligence, as with height, is not due to a single gene or even a few genes with simple dominant-recessive modes of inheritance. Instead, hundreds of genes are known that have a small effect on individual IQ scores. However, these small effects contribute to large genetic effects on IQ scores in the population as a whole.

Mendel's work led to the distinction between genotype and phenotype. Genotype refers to alleles, and phenotype refers to observed characteristics. For example, the genotype of a PKU carrier includes one normal allele and one PKU allele. Genotype and phenotype can differ, as in the case of a carrier of the PKU allele who does not have a PKU phenotype but has one PKU allele.

Of course, some phenotypic differences among people may have nothing to do with their genotypic differences. For example, although as many as a third of all our loci have varying alleles, these genotypic differences among us may not at all contribute to differences among us in some behavioral characteristic such as athletic ability, a trait that has not yet been studied by behavioral geneticists. The point of behavioral genetics is to assess the correspondence between genotypic differences and observed differences in behavior.

Mendel's work was rediscovered and explored further in the early part of the twentieth century. Some scientists doubted that Mendel's laws of heredity, which were based on pea plants, would apply to humans. The characteristics in the pea plant that Mendel studied were either-or (discontinuous or qualitative) traits, for instance, seeds that were either wrinkled or smooth. However, few such either-or traits are found in humans. In humans, most traits are normally distributed (continuous, quantitative), with most people in the middle and fewer and fewer as we go further above or below the mean. This controversy was resolved when Ronald Fisher and others noted that Mendel's mechanism of discrete inheritance also applies to normally distributed traits if we assume that many genes, each with a small effect, add up to produce observable differences among individuals in a population.

This is the fundamental point of quantitative genetic theory that underlies behavioral genetic research: the effects of many genes can add up to account for substantial variability in normally distributed traits. A single locus with two alleles produces three genotypes. When two loci are involved, nine genotypes occur; with three loci, there are 27 genotypes. The distribution quickly starts to look like a normal distribution, even when we assume that the alleles at the different loci equally affect the trait and that there is no environmental variation. Moreover, many genes have more than two alleles. As just mentioned, three loci with two alleles each yield 27 genotypes; with four alleles for each of 20 loci, the number of possible genotypes is 10 billion! Environmental variation, which is always important for behavioral phenotypes, also smooths out the distribution.

Genetic Influence and Behavior

Although we sometimes slip and talk about genes *for* something, like genes *for* height, we should talk about genetic influences on individual differences in height and on behavior. There are no genes for behavior just as there are no genes for beauty or athletic ability. Genes are chemical structures that can only code for amino acid sequences. These amino acid sequences interact with all of what we are and can thus indirectly affect endpoints as complex as behavior, but there is no gene for a particular behavior. For example, genetics appears to affect alcoholism but this does not mean there is a gene that makes us consume large quantities of alcohol. It may be that genetic factors influence our sensitivity to alcohol so that some of us need to drink more to get "high" and are for that reason at greater risk for alcoholism. Similarly, genetic effects on schizophrenia might involve a nervous system more sensitive to stress. All effects of genes on behavioral variability are indirect, representing the cumulative effects of stretches of amino acids that differ from person to person and that interact with the intracellular and extracellular environment. In this sense, genes do not determine behavior. What we are talking about is a probabilistic connection between genetic factors and behavioral differences among people.

Some genetic influences are more deterministic, although their effects on behavior are still indirect. For example, PKU can cause severe retardation because the DNA of this form of the gene codes for a defective enzyme that is unable to break down phenylalanine. Phenylalanine is a very common substance in our diets. If a child receives the defective gene on both chromosomes, she will not be able to produce the proper enzyme to break down phenylalanine. The phenylalanine consequently builds up, and this buildup is damaging to the developing brain, leading to severe retardation. Even though PKU is a single-gene trait, which can occur when two recessive PKU alleles are inherited, its cure is environmental. Retardation can be avoided if PKU is detected early and the amount of phenylalanine in the diet is restricted until the early school years, when the brain is sufficiently well developed that excess phenylalanine will not hurt it. This environmental engineering has been the remedy for this genetic defect since the 1950s, although questions remain about the causes and cures of PKU (Murphey, 1983).

Well over a thousand rare genes have been identified that may disrupt normal development, having impacts similar to the PKU gene. However, there are no known single genes that account for a significant portion of individual differences for any complex behavior. This is not surprising, considering the complexity of behavior. Molecular genetic research with organisms

as simple as bacteria makes it clear that many genes affect even
the simplest behaviors. For example, at least 40 genes are involved in the normal movement of bacteria. Any one of these
genes can seriously alter the bacteria's ability to move. Greater
complexity is added by the fact that any single gene can affect
many behaviors. The technical words for these two concepts
are *polygeny* and *pleiotropy*. Polygeny means that normal behavioral variation is influenced by many genes, each of which
contribute small portions of variability to the behavioral differences among individuals. Pleiotropy refers to the multiple,
indirect effects of genes on behavior. In other words, polygeny
means that one behavior can be influenced by many genes,
and pleiotropy means that one gene can affect many behaviors.

An example closer to home is the human brain. It has been
estimated that the adult brain contains 100 billion neurons
(nerve cells), each with approximately 1500 synapses that trans-
mit messages to and from the neurons. At each synapse there
are a million neurotransmitter molecules that could affect the
neuron. This complexity makes it implausible to think that differences among individuals in the activity of any neural system
are significantly determined by a single major gene.

In sum, any one of many genes can disrupt development,
but the normal range of behavioral variation is likely to be or-
chestrated by a system of many genes, each with small effect, as
well as by environmental influences. Each of the genes that
affect behavior are transmitted according to mechanisms of
heredity discovered by Mendel, and each of them are transcribed and translated according to the rules of molecular
genetics. The effects of polygenic influences on behavioral differences among people are no less genetic than are single-gene
effects. The effects are more complex, which is to be expected,
given the complexity of behavior.

In addition to polygeny and pleiotropy, a third factor that
plays a role is population. As indicated in the previous chapter,
genetic influence on behavior refers to the association between

genetic differences and behavioral differences among individuals in a particular population. These estimates of genetic influence are not constants like the speed of light; they are statistics that describe a particular population. Change the population—genetically or environmentally—and you change the result. Populations can obviously change environmentally for example, in relation to increasing access to education and mass media. If such changes had the effect of equalizing educational opportunity, differences among individuals would be smaller, but the differences that continued to exist would be due to an even greater extent to genetic differences. Genetic factors can also change. For example, migration can cause new genes to be introduced into a population, thereby increasing genetic variation in the population. Natural selection can curtail the reproduction of certain genotypes, thereby reducing genetic variation.

You might ask, "What good are estimates of genetic influence if they can change from population to population or from time to time?" The answer is that it is a reasonable first step in understanding any behavioral trait to ask the relative extent to which genetic differences and environmental differences in a particular population are responsible for observed differences among people. Moreover, behavioral genetic methods allow us to go beyond this first question to ask more refined questions about specific genetic and environmental influences.

It is important to emphasize that behavioral genetics describes "what is." Behavioral genetics does not tell us "what could be" if we were to change either genetic or environmental factors in the population. Moreover, behavioral genetics is not concerned with what should be. "What should be" implies values, and values should not direct science. Finding genetic influences on behavior is compatible with a wide range of social action, including no action at all. For example, great concern was generated during the 1970s when there was found to be substantial genetic influence on IQ scores (see Chapter 4).

However, this finding has no necessary consequences for social policy. Depending on one's values, one could use these findings to argue that educational resources should be primarily devoted to those children at the low end of the IQ distribution in an attempt to equalize IQ scores.

A concern of some is that genetic influences counsel despair—that nothing can be done to alter genetic effects. As an antidote to this concern, it could be argued that the more that is known about a trait genetically as well as environmentally, the more likely it is that rational intervention and prevention strategies can be devised. This is especially the case as we come to realize that many behavioral problems, such as psychopathology and alcoholism, cannot be effectively treated by means of rehabilitation after the problems become full blown. The ultimate solution must lie in primary prevention, an attempt to identify individuals at risk with the goal of preventing problems before they appear. PKU is a classic example in which discovery of the genetic basis for this type of mental retardation led to an environmentally mediated prevention strategy. Alcoholism, one of our most serious societal problems, is another example of a genetically influenced condition that could be prevented through environmental means. The discovery of genetic influence permits identification of some individuals at risk for alcoholism: if you have a first-degree relative who is alcoholic, you have a one-in-four risk of becoming alcoholic. Explaining the implications of such research could be an important "low-tech" intervention for this important societal problem, especially because you cannot become alcoholic unless you consume large amounts of alcohol.

This chapter explained what it means to say that genes influence behavior. The following chapter describes the methods used by behavioral geneticists to assess the extent of genetic influence on behavior.

Resources

Molecular Genetics

The tremendous advances in genetics have led to the publication of many books and textbooks on the topic. A highly readable account of the discovery of DNA structure and function is by one of its discoverers, James D. Watson (*The double helix*, New York: Atheneum, 1968). See also H. F. Judson (*The eighth day of creation: Makers of the revolution in biology*, New York: Simon & Schuster, 1986). The discovery of recombinant DNA techniques used so widely in modern molecular genetic research is described in *The DNA story* by James D. Watson and John Tooze (San Francisco: W. H. Freeman, 1981). These techniques are described in greater detail in *Recombinant DNA: A short course* by James D. Watson, John Tooze, and David T. Kurtz (New York: Scientific American Books, 1983).

Transmission Genetics

A lively general account of Mendelian genetics from an evolutionary perspective is *Heredity, evolution and society* by I. M. Lerner and W. J. Libby (San Franciso: W. H. Freeman, 1976). It is also interesting to read Gregor Mendel's original 1866 account, which is reprinted in translation in many places (for example, E. O. Dodson, *Genetics*, Philadelphia: Saunders, 1956).

3

How Can Genetic Influence on Behavior Be Detected?

The main purpose of this chapter is to describe the methods of behavioral genetics that make it possible to detect genetic influence on behavior. However, behavioral genetics is more than a set of methods. It represents a general perspective for the social and behavioral sciences, focusing on behavioral differences among individuals. Behavioral genetics also recognizes the possibility that genetic differences among people, in addition to environmental variations, can contribute to differences in behavior. The value of this perspective is that it represents a balanced view that considers nature as well as nurture in the study of individual differences. For this reason, the chapter begins with a brief discussion of quantitative genetic theory, which underlies the methods used in behavioral genetics.

Quantitative Genetic Theory

Quantitative genetics refers to the study of traits influenced by many genes as well as environmental factors. The origins of quantitative genetics in the early part of this century provide a useful introduction to the theory.

As explained in Chapter 2, Mendel discovered that heredity involves pairs of discrete units called genes. One gene from each pair is inherited from the mother and the other from the father. Mendel demonstrated this in experiments involving either-or traits (such as yellow versus green seeds) of pea plants that are determined by a single gene, with no important environmental variation. When Mendel's findings were rediscovered in the early 1900s, an important disagreement emerged, as mentioned in Chapter 2. A group called Mendelians looked for simple Mendelian patterns of single-gene inheritance. Their opponents, who were called biometricians, felt that Mendel's laws were not applicable to the complex characteristics of higher organisms. They argued instead that these complex traits, including behavior, are nearly always distributed quantitatively in a normal, bell-shaped curve, not in the either-or qualitative manner characteristic of the pea plants studied by Mendel.

Both sides were right and wrong. The Mendelians were correct in arguing that heredity works the way Mendel said it worked, but they were wrong in assuming that complex characteristics will show simple Mendelian patterns of inheritance. The biometricians were right in arguing that complex characteristics are distributed quantitatively, not qualitatively, but they were wrong in arguing that Mendel's laws of inheritance did not apply to higher organisms. The controversy was resolved when biometricians realized that Mendel's laws of the inheritance of single genes also apply to complex characteristics if we assume that many genes, each with a small effect, along with environmental factors, combine to produce differences among individuals. Behavioral research requires such a polygenic (multigene) approach because the complexity of behavior makes it unlikely that any single gene accounts for a substantial portion of the variance in the population. Although single-gene effects can be devastating for affected individuals, such as the severe mental retardation caused by untreated PKU, no single gene has been shown to account for detectable variance in the normal range of individual differences. Environmental variation is always potentially important as well.

Although the theory and its methods are usually presented in a sophisticated manner, the basic idea is simple. The theory of quantitative genetics involves four fundamental propositions. First, genetic differences among individuals can lead to phenotypic (observed) differences. Second, nongenetic (environmental) differences among individuals can also produce phenotypic differences. Third, if genetic differences are important for a particular trait, phenotypic similarity among relatives should vary according to their genetic similarity. This proposition leads directly to methods, described later, that can identify the genetic and environmental components of variance that underlie phenotypic variation. The fourth proposition is that if shared environmental factors influence a particular trait, phenotypic similarity will also produce similarity among relatives who have lived together.

The third proposition concerning genetic relatedness requires explanation. Quantitative genetic theory quantifies the degree of resemblance expected for different types of family relationships. The genetic relatedness of identical twins is 100 percent: they are essentially clones from a genetic point of view. At the other extreme are genetically unrelated individuals adopted into the same family: their genetic relatedness is zero.

Box 3.1
Statistics: Variance and Correlation

Although we have talked about individual differences using terms such as *variability, variance* can be used to describe more precisely the differences among individuals. Variance is based on each individual's difference from the average of the sample. Because the average deviation from the mean is zero, the variance statistic squares these deviations from the mean and then averages them. In other words, variance is the average squared deviation from the mean and is expressed in terms of squared units of measurement.

The square root of variance, called the *standard deviation,* is more easily understood. Differences among individuals are nearly always distributed as a bell-shaped curve (called a *normal distribution*) in which most people have scores near the middle of the distribution, and fewer and fewer individuals are found farther away from the average (see Figure 3.1). One standard deviation above (or below) the mean of a normal distribution is a score that is above (or below) about 84 percent of the individuals in the distribution; two stan-

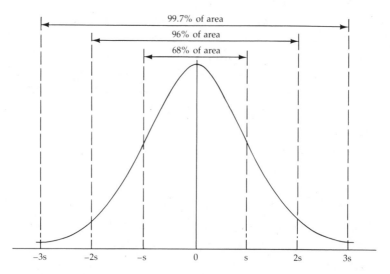

Figure 3.1. Normal distribution. The standard deviation (s) is the square root of variance. One standard deviation above the mean (the 50 percent score) represents a score at the 84th percentile (50 percent + 0.5 [68 percent] = 84 percent).

dard deviations is the 96th percentile. For example, IQ scores are normally distributed, as shown in Figure 3.2. IQ scores are adjusted to have a mean of 100 and a variance of 225. Thus, the standard deviation of IQ scores is 15 (the square root of 225), which means that if you have an IQ score of 115, you are one standard deviation above the mean, scoring higher than about 84 percent of individuals.

A correlation is a statistic that, in the case of behavioral genetic research, describes the proportion of variance that is shared, or "covaries," within pairs of individuals. The statistic goes from 0.00, indicating no resemblance, to 1.0, indicating perfect resemblance. Correlations can be negative, indicating dissimilarity, but this is rarely relevant in behavioral genetic research. Correlations can be seen most easily in terms of a plot between scores, for example between IQ scores for ten pairs of siblings, as in Figure 3.3. The correlation derived from these hypothetical data is 0.40. If the correlation were 1.0, all the points would be right on the line.

To get an intuitive feeling for correlations, consider that scores on

continued

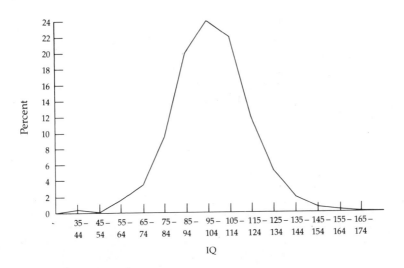

Figure 3.2. The distribution of IQ scores for children from 2 to 18 years of age. IQ scores are adjusted to have a mean of 100 and a standard deviation of 15 (from Terman & Merrill, 1973).

As discussed in the previous chapter, the focus is on genetic *differences*. Although all human beings share a great amount of identical DNA, the issue is to what extent variable (*polymorphic*) genes are shared by two individuals. In between the extremes of identical twins and genetically unrelated individuals are first-degree relatives—parents and their offspring and siblings—whose average degree of genetic relatedness is 50 per-

---

Box 3.1 *continued*
Statistics: Variance and Correlation

IQ tests correlate about 0.90 with scores on IQ tests taken by the same individuals a week later, that IQ scores when children enter school

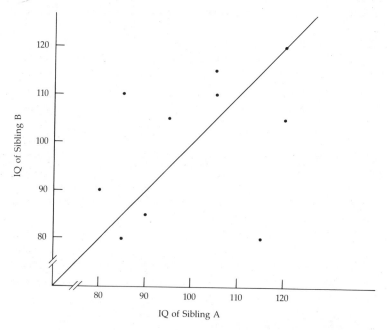

Figure 3.3. Plot of the association between IQ scores for ten sibling pairs. The sibling IQ correlation for these hypothetical data is 0.40.

cent. Fraternal twins are siblings in which two eggs are separately fertilized at the same time. This is in contrast to identical twins who develop from the same fertilized egg that splits into two zygotes during the first few days of life. Half siblings, who have only one parent in common, and other second-degree relatives are genetically related 25 percent. Third-degree relatives, such as cousins, are genetically related only 12.5 percent.

---

correlate about 0.50 with their IQ scores as adults, and that spouses correlate about 0.30 for IQ. Like variance, correlations are based on differences from the mean. Correlations for relatives are computed by taking each person's deviation from the mean, multiplying it by the relative's deviation from the relative's mean, and averaging these cross-products across all pairs of relatives. This is a statistic called *covariance*, which, like variance, is in squared units of measurement; a correlation is derived by dividing the covariance by the variance. Thus, a correlation is a proportion of the variance that covaries between relatives. For example, for IQ, the covariance between siblings is about 90; the variance of IQ scores is 225, and the correlation is about 0.40. This correlation of 0.40 indicates that 40 percent of the variance of IQ scores covaries among siblings.

In the social and behavioral sciences, the usual correlation is called an *interclass correlation* because it correlates two different things, such as height and weight. In behavioral genetics, the interclass correlation may be appropriate when we correlate two clear "classes" of relatives, such as parents and offspring. But what about twins for whom it is not clear which is twin A and which is twin B? In this case, a special type of correlation is usually reported, the *intraclass correlation*. This type of correlation is the same as the interclass correlation except that it takes into account all possible combinations of twin A and twin B for each pair so that it does not matter which twin is designated as twin A or twin B.

When behaviors such as mental illness or retardation are assessed in terms of whether an individual is affected or not, concordances rather than correlations are used, as explained in Box 3.2.

If simple additive genetic differences among individuals completely account for observed differences among individuals for a particular trait, correlations for a perfectly reliable measure of that trait would be 1.0 for identical twins, 0.50 for first-degree relatives, 0.25 for second-degree relatives, and 0.00 for pairs of genetically unrelated individuals. (See Box 3.1 for a description of correlations and variance.) This pattern of results for

---

Box 3.2
Statistics: Concordance

Concordance is used to express the risk of relatives of affected individuals for traits that are measured in an either-or way—that is, either affected or normal—as is the case for most illnesses such as mental illness, retardation, or diseases. Concordance is simply the proportion of pairs of relatives in which both members are affected. For example, if we studied 100 siblings of schizophrenics and found that ten siblings are also schizophrenic, the concordance for schizophrenia is 10 percent. In other words, siblings of schizophrenics have a one in ten chance (risk) of being schizophrenic.

In the case of twins, a different calculation of concordance is preferred if each affected member of a twin pair is identified independently. Instead of calculating the proportion of twin pairs in which both members are affected, the proportion of affected individuals (probands) is calculated. For this reason, the former

calculation is called *pairwise concordance*, and the latter method is called *probandwise concordance*. For example, consider the case in which 15 affected twin individuals were found who turned out to be members of ten pairs of twins. In other words, five pairs are concordant (ten affected individuals), and five pairs are discordant (five affected individuals). The pairwise concordance is 50 percent (five of ten pairs), but the probandwise concordance is 75 percent (15 of 20 individuals). The probandwise concordance is preferred because it can be compared to risk figures for other family groups and to general population rates; it permits us to express concordance in terms of the risk of the cotwin of an affected twin.

Concordances for relatives need to be compared to population prevalences of the disorder or to other comparison groups to determine whether there is resemblance. For schizophrenia, for example, first-a particular trait could only be explained by concluding that all of the variance for the trait is due to genetic variance in the population. A statistic describing the proportion of phenotypic variance due to genetic variance is *heritability;* in this example, heritability is 1.0. In the behavioral sciences, however, we have no examples of traits with heritabilities even close to 1.0. What pattern of correlations would occur if heredity accounts

---

degree relatives show concordances of about 8 percent, whereas the population incidence is about 1 percent, which indicates an eightfold increased risk for schizophrenia for first-degree relatives of schizophrenics. The problem with the concordance statistic is that it is difficult to interpret concordance in terms of variance explained by familial resemblance. A special type of correlation called phi incorporates the population incidence and familial concordance for either-or traits (Guilford & Fruchter, 1973). The phi coefficient can be interpreted much like the usual correlation, which is referred to as the Pearson (after Galton's student who developed the statistic) product-moment correlation.

Researchers often convert concordances to a special type of correlation that assumes that a normal distribution of liability (risk) underlies the either-or diagnosis (Falconer, 1965). For example, suppose we lost all our rulers and had to measure height in terms of a diagnosis of

"tall" based on individuals hitting their heads when passing through a certain doorway. One percent of the population hits their heads; first-degree relatives are 10 percent concordant for this tallness diagnosis. If we assume that the genetic and environmental factors that affect height are normally distributed, then the correlation for family members is greater than indicated by the 10 percent concordance, because many family members of "affected" tall individuals will just barely pass through the doorway without hitting their heads. A liability correlation of 0.45 can be estimated to describe this case, although two points should be emphasized: (1) many assumptions need to be made in order to calculate such a correlation from familial and population risk figures, and (2) this correlation refers to a hypothesized construct of liability for tallness rather than the observed characteristic of height per se.

for half of the variation for a particular trait? If sharing the same family environment does not increase the resemblance of family members for this trait, the expected correlations would be half those listed above: 0.50 for identical twins, 0.25 for first-degree relatives, 0.125 for second-degree relatives, and 0.00 for pairs of genetically unrelated individuals. Finally, if these correlations all turned out to be near zero for a particular trait, we could safely conclude that heredity is unimportant for the trait.

To reiterate, the third proposition of quantitative genetics is that expected phenotypic similarity among relatives varies according to their genetic similarity. The fourth proposition is that shared environments can also produce similarity among relatives living together. However, in all the relationships just described, family members share environment but differ in their genetic relatedness. Thus, if heredity is important for a particular trait, identical twins will be more similar than siblings, who will, in turn, be more similar than half siblings, who will be more similar than adoptive siblings. Nonetheless, some portion of the similarity of family members living together can be due to shared environment. As discussed later, this shared environment component of variance can be estimated, for example, by the resemblance between genetically unrelated individuals reared together in the same adoptive family.

These four propositions lead directly to the methods used in behavioral genetic research. Although human methods are emphasized in this book, it is helpful to begin with a brief discussion of methods that can be used with animals.

Behavioral Genetic Methods Used in Animal Studies

The two major methods used in animal studies are strain studies and selection studies. Strain studies compare inbred strains in which brothers have been mated with sisters for at least 20 generations. This intensive inbreeding makes each animal within the strain virtually a clone of all other members of the strain. In genetic research with mammals, mice are most often studied, and over 100 inbred strains of mice are available. Because inbred strains differ genetically from each other, genetically influenced traits will show average differences between inbred strains reared in the same laboratory environment, whereas differences within strains estimate environmental influences. Strain studies have been important in suggesting that most mouse behaviors show genetic influence.

Selection studies provide the clearest evidence for genetic influence: if a trait is heritable, you can select for it, as animal breeders have known for centuries. Laboratory experiments typically select high and low lines in addition to maintaining an unselected control line. For example, the largest and longest selection study of mice was conducted by John DeFries of the University of Colorado. Mice were selected who were the most active in an open field, and these mice were mated with each other. The least active mice were also mated with each other. From the offspring of the high-active mice, the most and least active mice were selected and mated in a similar manner. The results of this selection study are shown in Figure 3.4 for replicated high, low, and control lines. The steadily increasing difference between the high and low lines indicates many genes affecting open-field activity. As illustrated in Figure 3.5, after 30 generations of such selective breeding, a thirtyfold average difference in activity has been bred: there is no overlap between the activity of the low and high lines. The high-active mice now run the equivalent total distance of the length of a football field during two three-minute test periods in the open-field apparatus, while the low-active mice sit on the sidelines.

· Selection studies such as these have confirmed the conclusion from strain studies that heredity influences individual differences in many mouse behaviors.

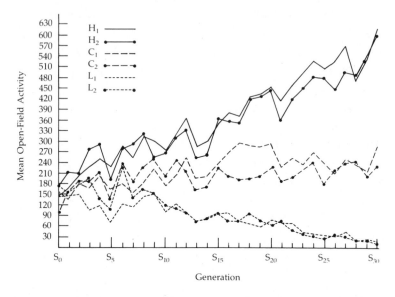

Figure 3.4. Results of a selection study of open-field activity. Two lines were selected for high open-field activity (H_1 and H_2), two lines were selected for low open-field activity (L_1 and L_2), and two lines were randomly mated within line to serve as controls (C_1 and C_2). (From "Response to 30 generations of selection for open-field activity in laboratory mice" by J. C. DeFries, M. C. Gervais, and E. A. Thomas, *Behavior Genetics*, 8:3–13. Copyright © 1978 by Plenum Publishing Corporation. All rights reserved.)

Human Behavioral Genetic Methods

Family Designs

In studies of human beings for whom selection studies or comparisons among inbred strains cannot be conducted, it is necessary to study pairs of individuals that differ in genetic resemblance. As indicated earlier, if heredity is important for a particular trait, pairs of individuals that are more similar genetically ought to be more similar for the trait. If heredity does not affect the trait, differences in genetic similarity should not affect the resemblance of these pairs of individuals.

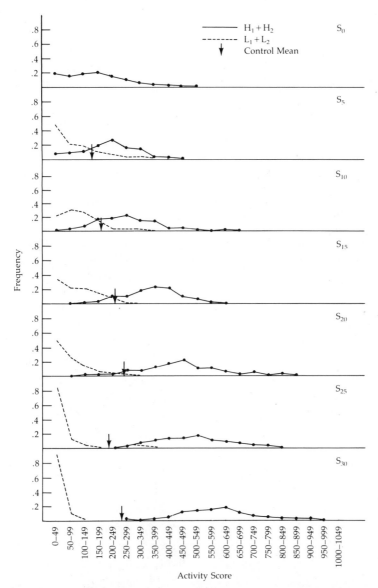

Figure 3.5. Distributions of activity scores of lines selected for high and low open-field activity. Average activity of control lines in each generation is indicated by an arrow. (From "Response to 30 generations of selection for open-field activity in laboratory mice" by J. C. DeFries, M. C. Gervais, and E. A. Thomas, *Behavior Genetics*, 8:3–13. Copyright © 1978 by Plenum Publishing Corporation. All rights reserved.)

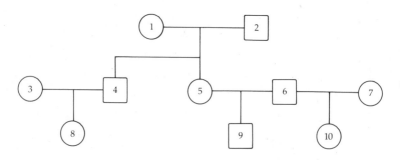

Figure 3.6. Pedigree (family tree) illustrating genetic relatedness. Females are indicated by circles and males by squares; 1 and 2 are married, and 4 and 5 are their children who have married individuals 3 and 6. First-degree relatives (50 percent genetically related) include parents and offspring (1 and 4) and siblings (4 and 5). Second-degree relatives (25 percent genetically related) are one step removed: grandparents and their grandchildren (1 and 8), aunts/uncles and their nieces/nephews (5 and 8), and half siblings who have only one parent in common (9 and 10) typically because parents divorce and remarry (6). Cousins (8 and 9) are third-degree relatives (12.5 percent genetically related).

The problem with this approach is that environmental resemblance usually goes along with genetic relatedness. For example, cousins, half siblings, and full siblings are likely to share increasingly similar environments. Because relatives often share environment as well as heredity, familial resemblance can be due to environmental influences as well as to hereditary influences. Nonetheless, family studies are useful for estimating the limits of genetic and environmental influences. For example, if first-degree relatives do not resemble each other for a particular trait, then neither shared heredity nor shared family environment affect the trait. As explained earlier, if they correlate 0.25 for the trait, heritability is likely to be no greater than 50 percent, although heritability could be much lower if shared environment accounts for familial resemblance for the trait.

The two major methods for studying human behavioral genetics were designed to determine the extent to which familial resemblance is due to shared heredity or shared environment. These are the adoption method and the twin method, which are discussed below.

Adoption Designs

Again, the basic problem in family studies is that resemblance among relatives could be due either to shared heredity or to shared environment. The adoption design severs these two sources of familial resemblance: genetically related individuals adopted apart and reared in uncorrelated environments will resemble each other only for genetic reasons, and genetically unrelated individuals adopted together into the same family will resemble each other only for reasons of shared environment. In this way, the degree of resemblance between adopted-apart relatives reveals the impact of heredity, and the resemblance between adopted-together individuals assesses the importance of shared environment.

The simplest adoption design to understand is the rare, but dramatic, situation in which identical twins are adopted separately at birth and reared apart in uncorrelated environments. The resemblance of these pairs, expressed as a correlation, can be attributed to heredity. For example, the correlation for reared-apart identical twins for height is about 0.90. (See Box 3.3 concerning the interpretation of correlations.) This implies that about 90 percent of the variation in height is shared by reared-apart identical twins. (As explained in Box 3.3, correlations inform us about proportions of variance.) Most important, this resemblance—unlike the resemblance for identical twins reared together—cannot be due to shared environment, because the twins were adopted apart and lived in different, uncorrelated families. If we studied pseudopairs of genetically unrelated individuals picked at random from the population, their correlation would be close to zero. Thus, the correlation for height for adopted-apart identical twins suggests substantial genetic causation of individual differences in height. As mentioned earlier, heritability is a statistic that

Box 3.3
Interpreting Correlations

One of the things you learn in an elementary statistics course is that correlations do not imply causation. This means that a correlation merely involves an association and does not imply that one thing causes the other. Across cities, the amount of alcohol consumed and the number of churches are highly correlated, but this is not because one causes the other. Rather, more alcohol is consumed and more churches are built in large cities than in small cities. In contrast, behavioral genetic designs such as the adoption design are natural experiments, and the correlations derived from these experiments do imply causation. For example, the correlation for identical twins adopted apart into uncorrelated environments estimates genetic influence—how else can we explain the twins' similarity?

Another rule from statistics that needs to be unlearned concerns the variation accounted for by a correlation. For a correlation between two variables, such as the correlation of 0.60 between height and weight, we are taught to square the correlation in order to estimate the amount of variation in weight that can be accounted for by variation in height (or vice versa). The answer is that 36 percent (that is, 0.60×0.60) of the variation in weight is related to variation in height. However, in behavioral genetics, the issue is not how much of the variation in identical twins reared apart can be predicted by knowledge of the variation of the twin partners but rather the proportion of variance shared by the twins that is given by the correlation itself rather than the square of the correlation. In other words, a correlation of 0.60 for identical twins reared apart for a particular measure indicates that 60 percent of the variance for that measure is shared by identical twins reared apart.

One other issue concerning the interpretation of correlations is that like all statistics, they involve a margin of error and need to be evaluated in terms of statistical significance. Error is a function of sample size and the size of the correlation. The usual rule of thumb is that a correlation is said to be statistically significant if it would occur by chance fewer than one in 20 times. By this rule, a correlation of 0.25 would be statistically significant if it were based on a sample size of at least 45 pairs of individuals; a correlation of 0.50 would be statistically significant if the sample size were at least 12 pairs. The need for large samples is discussed further in Box 3.5.

quantifies the extent of genetic influence. (See Box 3.4 for a discussion of heritability.) In the case of identical twins reared apart, their correlation directly represents heritability; in other words, the correlation of 0.90 suggests that 90 percent of the variation in height is due to genetic variation. It cannot be

---

Box 3.4
Heritability

As indicated in the text, heritability is a statistic that describes the proportion of phenotypic variance due to genetic variance. In addition to indicating whether genetic influence is significant, behavioral genetic methods can be used to estimate the extent of genetic influence, namely, heritability. Box 3.1 indicates that a correlation is a statistic that describes the proportion of phenotypic variance due to covariance. In the case of identical twins adopted apart in uncorrelated environments, their correlation represents the proportion of phenotypic variance (Vp) due to genetic variance (Vg) that covaries between identical twins adopted apart:

$$\text{Correlation for identical twins reared apart} = \frac{Vg}{Vp} = \text{heritability}$$

That is, they covary only for genetic reasons. For this reason the correlation for identical twins reared apart directly estimates heritability. In the height example in the text, the correlation for adopted-apart identical twins is 0.90, suggesting that herita-

bility is 90 percent—that is, 90 percent of the phenotypic variance in height is due to genetic differences among individuals.

What about adopted-apart first-degree relatives? Their correlation also represents the extent to which phenotypic variance covaries; however, their covariance includes only half the genetic effects, because first-degree relatives are only similar 50 percent genetically:

$$\text{Correlation for adopted-apart first-degree relatives} = \frac{0.50Vg}{Vp} = 0.50 \text{ heritability}$$

Thus, their correlation estimates one-half of heritability; the correlation is doubled to estimate heritability. For the example of height, the correlation for adopted-apart first-degree relatives is 0.45; doubling this correlation yields an estimate of 90 percent heritability for height, the same estimate as above.

Unlike adopted-apart relatives, other behavioral genetic designs involve shared environment as well as
continued

overemphasized that heritability refers to individual differences in a population, *not* to a single individual. The heritability of height does not mean that you grew to 90 percent of your height for reasons of heredity and that the other inches were added by environment. What it does mean is that most of the height

---

Box 3.4 *continued*
Heritability

shared heredity, which makes the estimation of heritability somewhat more complicated. Consider the adoption design that compares non-adoptive and adoptive families. Non-adoptive parents and their offspring share family environment in addition to their 50 percent genetic similarity, so that their covariance includes the influence of shared environment as well as half of the genetic influence. However, adoptive parents and their adopted children share only family environment. The difference in correlations for nonadoptive and adoptive parents and offspring involves the following components of variance:

$$\underset{\text{(nonadoptive)}}{\frac{0.50Vg + Ve}{Vp}} - \underset{\text{(adoptive)}}{\frac{Ve}{Vp}} = \frac{0.50Vg}{Vp}$$

$$= 0.50 \text{ heritability}$$

Doubling the difference in nonadoptive and adoptive correlations estimates heritability. For height, the correlations are 0.45 and 0.00, respectively; heritability is again estimated as 90 percent.

In the twin method, heritability is also estimated from the differ-

ence between correlations. For twins reared together, the covariance for identical twins includes all genetic influence plus shared environment, and the covariance for fraternal twins includes half the genetic influence plus shared environment. The difference in correlations again estimates half the heritability:

$$\underset{\text{(identical)}}{\frac{Vg + Ve}{Vp}} - \underset{\text{(fraternal)}}{\frac{0.50Vg + Ve}{Vp}} = \frac{0.50Vg}{Vp}$$

$$= 0.50 \text{ heritability}$$

Doubling the difference between identical and fraternal twin correlations estimates heritability. For height, identical and fraternal twin correlations are 0.90 and 0.45, respectively; heritability is again estimated as 90 percent.

Box 3.6 (p. 61) illustrates the relationship between such correlations and heritability in terms of path analysis. Table 3.1 (p. 65) provides some hypothetical examples of family, twin, and adoption correlations so you can work through the estimation of heritability. Complications in the estimation of heritability are discussed later.

differences among people are due to the genetic differences among them.

Identical twins reared apart are rare; all the world's literature adds up to fewer than 100 pairs. (However, one ongoing study in America and two studies using nationwide records of twins in Scandinavia are tripling that number; more will be heard about this design and these data in the future.) Nonetheless, other adoption designs involving first-degree relatives are useful. Most of these studies investigate the resemblance between biological parents and their offspring who were relinquished for adoption at birth. Adopted-apart siblings can also be used to assess the influence of heredity.

Because first-degree relatives resemble each other only 50 percent genetically, the correlation for adopted-apart first-degree relatives for a trait such as height includes only half of the genetic variance. The other half of the genetic variance

Figure 3.7. The "Jim twins" (James Springer and James Lewis), identical twins adopted apart at birth and unaware of each other for 40 years until they were reunited as part of the Minnesota Study of Twins Reared Apart (Thomas S. England/Photo Researchers Inc.)

that affects the trait makes first-degree relatives different. That is, if a trait were perfectly heritable, the observed correlation for adopted-apart first-degree relatives would be 0.50, not 1.0 as in the case of identical twins. Thus, if a correlation of 0.50 is observed for adopted-apart first-degree relatives, we would estimate heritability as 1.0. In other words, correlations for adopted-apart first-degree relatives need to be doubled in order to estimate heritability. Using height as an example, the observed correlation for adopted-apart parents and offspring is about 0.45, suggesting again that about 90 percent of the variation in height among individuals is genetic in origin.

In addition to studying genetically related individuals who are adopted apart, the other part of the adoption design investigates resemblance for a particular trait among genetically unrelated individuals living in the same adoptive family. Adoptive parents and their adopted children provide a test of the contribution of shared family environment to parent-offspring resemblance. Also, the correlation for genetically unrelated children adopted into the same home assesses the role of shared environment in sibling resemblance.

The full adoption design evaluates genetic influence by observing the resemblance of adopted-apart relatives and assesses shared environmental influence via the resemblance of adopted individuals who are genetically unrelated but reared together. Another adoption design estimates genetic influence indirectly by comparing nonadoptive families to adoptive families. For example, nonadoptive parent-offspring resemblance could be due to heredity or to shared environment; adoptive parent-offspring resemblance can be due only to shared environment. If heredity is important for a particular trait, nonadoptive parent-offspring resemblance will exceed resemblance for adoptive parents and their adopted children.

The major potential problem with the adoption design is selective placement, the placement of adopted-apart relatives into environments that are correlated for characteristics that affect the trait under study. For example, if adopted-apart identical twins are actually reared in homes similar with respect to factors that affect IQ (such as socioeconomic status), then their IQ resemblance could to some extent be brought about by their environmental similarity rather than by their genetic similarity alone. Similarly, if adoptive parents are matched to biological parents, genetic influence could inflate the correlation between adoptive parents and their adopted children, and environmental influence could inflate the correlation between biological parents and their adopted-away children. Fortunately, some adoption studies show little or no selective placement. However, if selective placement is found in an adoption study, its effects need to be considered in interpreting results.

The Twin Method

The other major method compares correlations for identical and fraternal twins reared together. As noted earlier, identical twins are genetically identical, whereas fraternal twins, like other first-degree relatives, resemble each other only 50 percent genetically. Identical twins are sometimes called monozygotic (MZ) because they derive from one zygote; fraternal twins are called dizygotic (DZ). Although resemblance between first-degree and second-degree relatives could also be compared as a test of the importance of hereditary similarity, the twin method has two major advantages as a natural experiment. First, the difference in genetic relatedness is greater between identical and fraternal twins (100 percent for identical twins versus 50 percent for fraternal twins) than between first- and second-degree relatives (50 percent versus 25 percent). Second, both identical and fraternal twins share the same womb, are born at the same time, and live in the same family. In contrast, first- and second-degree relatives differ in age, and second-degree relatives typically live in different families.

The essence of the twin method is the comparison of correlations for the two types of twins. If a trait is not influenced by heredity, identical twins should be no more similar for the trait than fraternal twins, despite the twofold greater genetic similarity of identical twins. If heredity is important, however, identical twins will resemble each other to a greater extent than will fraternal twins. For example, height yields an identical twin correlation of about 0.90 and a fraternal twin correlation of about 0.45, suggesting, not surprisingly, substantial genetic influence on individual differences in height. Because the identical twin correlation is significantly greater than the fraternal twin correlation, genetic influence for height is statistically significant.

We can also estimate heritability, the magnitude of genetic influence, by doubling the difference between the identical and fraternal twin correlations, as explained in Box 3.4. The reason for this should be apparent. Genetic similarity for identical and fraternal twins is 100 percent and 50 percent, respectively. The difference, then, between identical and fraternal twin correlations contains only half of the genetic effect. Doubling the difference between the two correlations estimates all of the genetic effect, the proportion of phenotypic variance that can be accounted for by genetic factors, which is referred to as heritability. In the case of height, doubling the difference between identical and fraternal twin correlations yields a heritability estimate of 0.90 (that is, $2(0.90 - 0.45) = 0.90$), suggesting again that the major reason why people differ in height is genetic.

Twins are more common than people usually realize—about one in 85 births are twins. Moreover, the numbers of identical twins and same-sex fraternal twins are approximately equal. That is, of all twins, about one-third are identical twins, one-third are same-sex fraternal twins, and the other third are opposite-sex fraternal twins. Because identical twins are always of the same sex, twin studies typically use same-sex fraternal twins for comparison with identical twins. How can you tell if same-sex twins are identical or fraternal? Single-gene markers assessed from blood can accurately answer the question: if a pair of twins has any different alleles, the pair must be fraternal. The chance that two people other than identical twins will have identical alleles at a dozen polymorphic loci is extremely small.

Physical characteristics can be used in the same way to determine whether twins are identical or fraternal. Highly heritable traits, such as eye color and hair color and texture, are affected by many genes. If a pair of twins is identical for several such characteristics, it is nearly certain that the pair must be identical twins. In fact, a single question works pretty well because it incorporates numerous polygenic characteristics: When the twins were young, how difficult were they to tell apart for strangers, friends, and relatives? To be mistaken for another person requires that many heritable characteristics such as hair, eyes, and body type are identical. Physical similarity approaches have been shown to be at least 95 percent accurate when compared to blood diagnoses. The availability of twins and the ease of diagnosing whether they are identical or fraternal are important issues, because large numbers of twin pairs are needed to assess genetic influence, as explained in Box 3.5. The reason for this is that the twin method relies on the difference between two correlations, and differences in correlations have large errors of estimation.

As mentioned earlier, selective placement is a possible problem with the adoption design. With the twin method, the so-called equal environments assumption could be a problem. That is, if identical twins are treated more similarly for nongenetic reasons than are fraternal twins, greater behavioral resemblance of identical twins could be due to environment rather than heredity. Behavioral genetic researchers have studied this issue, and it appears that the assumption of equal environments for the two types of twins is reasonable for most traits (Plomin, DeFries & McClearn, 1989).

Refinements of the Adoption and Twin Designs

In our discussion of the adoption and twin designs, some assumptions were made to simplify the presentation so that the gist of these natural experiments would be more easily understood. The purpose of this section is to discuss these assumptions: nonadditive genetic variance, assortative mating, and genotype-environment correlation and interaction.

Nonadditive genetic variance. Geneticists distinguish two types of genetic effects on a particular trait: additive and nonadditive. In the analysis of human behavior, nearly all

---

Box 3.5
Large Samples Needed

Behavioral genetic designs require large samples in order to estimate genetic and environmental parameters in the population. These estimates are based on correlations, which, like all statistics, involve errors of estimate that are a function of sample size and the size of the correlation. As indicated in Box 3.3, if the true correlation for identical twins reared apart were 0.50, we would need at least 12 pairs in order to show that the correlation—which directly estimates heritability—is statistically significant. Designs based on first-degree relatives will have lower correlations and thus require larger sample sizes. If heritability is 50 percent, as in the example for identical twins reared apart, the correlation for adopted-apart first-degree relatives would be 0.25. In this case, we would need at least 45 pairs to show statistical significance. The same issue is involved in correlations between genetically unrelated individuals adopted together used to

estimate the influence of shared environment.

Direct estimates that are based on a single correlation require smaller sample sizes than indirect methods in which one correlation is subtracted from another. For example, in one type of adoption design, genetic influence is estimated by subtracting an adoptive family correlation from a correlation for nonadoptive families. Similarly, in the case of the twin method, the difference between identical and fraternal twin correlations is the basis for estimating heritability. The difference between two correlations has a much larger error of estimation than does a single correlation. For example, if the correlation for a particular trait were 0.50 in nonadoptive families and 0.25 in adoptive families, we would need 65 nonadoptive pairs and 65 adoptive pairs to detect a significant difference in correlations of this magnitude. If genetic influence in the population is lower—that is, if genetic effects have been thought to operate in an additive manner. However, recent research is beginning to suggest that some traits, such as personality traits, may be influenced by nonadditive genetic effects. For this reason, this section describes the distinction and considers nonadditive genetic effects on adoption and twin methods.

Additive genetic variance refers to genetic effects that simply add up across genes. For example, the more "tallness"

---

the difference between the nonadoptive and adoptive correlations is smaller—much larger samples are needed to provide the statistical power necessary to find the difference.

Large samples are especially important when it comes to estimating heritability—a more demanding task, statistically speaking, than simply detecting the statistical significance of genetic influence. For example, if we found a correlation of 0.50 for adopted-apart identical twins in a sample of 12 pairs, we would estimate heritability to be 0.50. However, with this sample size there would only be about two chances out of three that the true value of heritability is between 0.28 and 0.67; we can be 95 percent certain only that the true heritability is between 0.00 and 0.84. If, however, we had 50 pairs, there would be two chances out of three that heritability is between 0.38 and 0.60; the 95 percent confidence interval is 0.26 to 0.68. Indirect designs require much larger sample sizes to obtain reasonably

powerful estimates of heritability. For example, suppose that the correlations for the two groups (nonadoptive versus adoptive relatives, or identical versus fraternal twins) are 0.50 and 0.25, which implies that heritability is 0.50 because we double the difference in correlations to estimate heritability. If the sample consisted of 65 pairs of each type, there would only be two out of three chances that the true heritability is between about 0.20 and 0.80; if 200 pairs of each type were studied, this confidence interval would shrink to a range of 0.33 to 0.67.

Two points should be taken from this discussion: large samples are needed, and heritability estimates, like all descriptive statistics, involve error of estimation. When we say that the heritability of a trait is 50 percent, this should not be taken too literally; we often only mean that it is between 30 and 70 percent.

alleles that you have, the taller you will be. Genetic effects that do not add up are called nonadditive. Nonadditive effects involve interactions among alleles at a single locus (dominance-recessiveness) as well as interactions among alleles at different loci (epistasis). The reason for this distinction is that additive genetic variance "breeds true" in the sense that children resemble their parents for a particular trait only to the extent that genetic effects on the trait are additive, as explained later. This has always been of practical concern to animal breeders, because nonadditive genetic variance will not respond to artificial selection. Offspring of selected parents will resemble their parents only to the extent that genetic variance is additive.

Dominance and recessiveness refer to interactions among alleles at a particular locus. Mendel referred to this phenomenon as dominance because one allele seems to dominate the expression of another allele. Consider a recessive disorder such as sickle-cell anemia. If you have one allele for sickle-cell anemia at the locus that codes for hemoglobin for red blood cells, you are a carrier but will not express sickle-cell anemia. In other words, the normal allele is dominant over the sickle-cell allele. Under normal circumstances you will not show the oxygen deprivation caused by the ineffective red blood cells of sickle-cell anemia. However, if your other allele at the locus is also a sickle-cell allele, the locus will eventually kill you, because you will not be able to produce fully functioning red blood cells. These alleles at the hemoglobin locus do not add up simply in their effect on the phenotype; none and one of these alleles show no effect, whereas two alleles produce a lethal effect. In other words, the alleles interact in their effect on the phenotype; if they added up in their effect, one allele would show some effect, and two alleles would yield a proportionately greater effect. In addition to interactions among alleles at a single locus, gene products at one locus can also interact with gene products at other loci. This type of nonadditive genetic effect is called *epistasis*.

If genetic effects are nonadditive, children will not resemble their parents, because children inherit only one of each pair of alleles from their parents. That is, if genetic effects are due to particular combinations of two alleles at the same locus or to special combinations of alleles at different loci, children cannot inherit these combinations. Siblings have a 25 percent chance of inheriting the same pair of alleles at a particular locus and thus resemble each other slightly for dominance effects. For most purposes, it is sufficient to say that siblings do not resemble each other genetically for epistatic interactions. Identical twins, however, are identical at all loci and thus resemble each other for all nonadditive genetic effects as well as for additive genetic effects.

If nonadditive genetic effects were important for a particular trait, the identical twin correlation would be high, but the correlation for first-degree relatives would be disproportionately low. That is, first-degree relatives would be less than half as similar as identical twins. Resemblance for adopted-apart identical twins includes both additive and nonadditive genetic variance and thus provides an accurate estimate of total genetic influence. An estimate like this is called *broad heritability* because it includes both additive and nonadditive genetic variance. Adoption designs based on adopted-apart first-degree relatives would underestimate the total genetic influence, because resemblance in these designs is the result only of additive genetic variance. Estimates such as these are called *narrow heritability* because they include only additive genetic variance. The twin method overestimates broad heritability in the presence of nonadditive genetic variance: the difference between identical and fraternal twin correlations properly includes half of the additive genetic variance (which is why we double the difference to estimate heritability) but includes nearly all of the nonadditive genetic variance. Thus, doubling the difference in twin correlations inflates broad heritability estimates to the extent that nonadditive genetic variance is important.

Assortative mating.   Another refinement of adoption and twin methods that needs to be considered is assortative mating, the tendency for spouses to be similar. Our earlier discussion of adoption and twin designs assumed that mating was random. This does not mean that people are sexually promiscuous but rather that people do not select mates similar to themselves in terms of the trait under study. In fact, spouses mate with positive assortment (that is, they are similar to one another), especially for physical characteristics, cognitive abilities, and, to a lesser extent, personality and psychopathology.

Assortative mating is important in two ways. First, it adds additive genetic variance into the population with each successive generation. For example, suppose that spouses mated at random with respect to height: a tall woman is just as likely to marry a short man as a tall man. Offspring will tend to be intermediate in height. However, because tall women tend to marry taller-than-average men, their offspring receive a double dose of the many genes involved in height and will be taller than expected if mating were random with respect to height. In this way, assortative mating spreads out the genetic variance in the population.

Second, assortative mating affects heritability estimates because it increases genetic resemblance between first-degree relatives. For example, resemblance between biological mothers and their adopted-away offspring is inflated because it indirectly includes some resemblance between the biological fathers and their adopted-away offspring in that biological mothers and fathers are similar. For this reason, adoption designs based on first-degree relatives will overestimate heritability somewhat if assortative mating is important. Identical twins, however, are genetically identical, and their genetic similarity cannot be increased by assortative mating. Thus, estimates of heritability based on correlations for adopted-apart identical twins are not affected by assortative mating. The twin method, however, underestimates genetic influence if assortative mating is a factor.

Assortative mating adds to the correlation for fraternal twins and thereby reduces the difference between the identical and fraternal twin correlations. Fortunately, it is easy to determine whether assortative mating is important merely by obtaining a correlation between spouses, and behavioral genetic analyses can be adjusted for its effect.

Genotype-environment correlation and interaction. Genotype-environment (GE) correlation literally refers to a correlation between genetic and environmental effects. It describes the extent to which children are exposed to environments on the basis of their genetic propensities. For example, if musical ability is heritable, then musically gifted children will have, on average, musically gifted parents who provide them with a musical environment as well as musical heritage. The children might be picked out as gifted and given special opportunities at school. Even if no one does anything about the child's talent, the child might gravitate toward musical environments. These three examples represent the three types of GE correlation: passive, reactive, and active, respectively.

GE interaction denotes an interaction in the statistical sense. The effect of environmental factors depends on genotype. For example, a particular approach to musical training might work well for children with at least moderate musical talent even though it is a dismal failure for other children.

These two concepts of GE correlation and interaction are quite different from the often-proposed idea that genetic and environmental influences cannot be studied separately because they "interact"—the belief that organisms' behavior is affected by both genes and environment. Of course, DNA in a void will not exhibit behavior nor will an environment without DNA. In this obvious sense, it is true that behavior cannot occur unless there is an organism to behave and an environment in which to behave, but this is not relevant to behavioral genetics. As emphasized in the previous chapter, behavioral genetics is the study of individual differences in a population, not the study of a single individual. Genetic differences among individuals can be important even when the environment does not vary substantially. Environmental differences can be important regardless of genetic effects. In addition to these direct effects, genetic and environmental influences can also correlate and interact.

GE correlation and interaction are important topics in their own right. They represent current directions in behavioral genetic research, especially attempts to identify specific GE correlations and interactions. In terms of the adoption and twin methods, we would like to obtain separate estimates of variance due to GE correlation and GE interaction, because these effects are neither genetic nor environmental effects but rather joint genetic-environmental effects. However, this is not possible yet except in the case of passive GE correlation that contributes to resemblance in nonadoptive families but not for adopted-apart or adopted-together relatives.

For this reason, we can only consider the effects of GE correlation and interaction on behavioral genetic analyses. Although adopted-apart individuals do not share passive GE correlation, others might react to adopted-apart individuals in similar ways because of their genetic similarity (reactive GE correlation). Also, adopted-apart relatives might seek or create similar environments that increase resemblance (active GE correlation). Thus, genetic estimates based on adopted-apart relatives do not include passive GE correlation but may include GE correlation of the reactive and active varieties. This is also the case for genetic estimates derived from comparisons between identical and fraternal twin correlations. The effects of GE interaction are not easily summarized. To the extent that GE interaction involves unique combinations of genotypes and environments, it will lower all familial correlations. This will lower genetic estimates based on adopted-apart relatives, although it will not affect the difference between identical and fraternal twin correlations.

Multivariate Analysis

An important advance in behavioral genetics in recent years is the extension of univariate analyses of the variance of a single trait to multivariate analysis of the covariance between traits (DeFries & Fulker, 1986).

In the past, behavioral geneticists studied genetic and environmental influences on the variance of one trait—for example, verbal ability—and then considered another trait, such as spatial ability. However, it is also possible to study genetic and environmental contributions to the covariance or correlation between traits. For example, what are the relative contributions of genetic and environment factors to the correlation between verbal ability and spatial ability? Between biology and behavior—such as correlations between heart rate measures and personality? Between behavior at one age and behavior at a later age? From a genetic perspective, a multivariate approach is important because it is highly unlikely that completely different sets of genes affect the various behaviors we examine. Multivariate analysis allows us to determine the overlap (pleiotropy) of genetic effects across behaviors.

The twin and adoption methods we have discussed in terms of analyzing the variance of single traits can easily be extended to the analyses of the covariance among traits in order to assess the extent to which genetic effects on one trait also affect other traits. The basic idea is that instead of analyzing correlations for twins or other family members, *cross-correlations* are analyzed. A cross-correlation is the correlation, say, between one twin's verbal ability and the other twin's spatial ability. Cross-correlations can be analyzed in the same way as correlations. For example, if identical twin cross-correlations exceed fraternal twin cross-correlations, genetic influence is implied. A multivariate analysis has been applied recently, for instance, to the study of diverse cognitive abilities (LaBuda, DeFries & Fulker, 1987). The analysis suggests that shared environmental factors affecting one cognitive ability are largely the same as shared environmental factors affecting other cognitive abilities. Genes affecting one measure, say vocabulary, within a cognitive ability factor (verbal) overlap substantially with genetic effects on other measures of that same ability, such as verbal analogies. However, genes affecting one specific cognitive ability (verbal) are not closely related to genes affecting another specific cognitive ability (spatial).

Combinations of Methods

During the past two decades, behavioral geneticists have begun to use designs that combine the family, adoption, and twin methods in order to bring more power to bear on their analyses. Two important combinations are adoption/family designs and adoption/twin designs. For example, in addition to studying "genetic" parents (biological parents and their adopted-away offspring) and "environmental" parents (adoptive parents and their adopted children), "genetic-plus-environmental" parents (nonadoptive families) represent an important addition to parent-offspring adoption designs. An example of the adoption/twin combination is the use of twins reared apart and twins reared together in the same study.

The twin and family methods can also be combined. For example, studying nontwin siblings reared together in addition to identical and fraternal twins provides a useful comparison between fraternal twins and nontwin siblings. It assesses the extent to which twins share more similar family environments than do nontwin siblings.

An interesting combination of the twin and family methods comes from the study of families of identical twins, which has come to be known as the families-of-twins method. When identical twins become adults and have their own children, interesting family relationships emerge. For example, in families of identical twins, nephews are as related genetically to their twin uncle as they are to their twin father. That is, in terms of their genetic relatedness, it is as if they have the same father. Similarly, cousins (third-degree relatives) are as closely related as half-siblings (second-degree relatives).

Model Fitting

A major development in behavioral genetics during the past decade is the testing of explicit models rather than the simple examination of correlations. This technique is especially useful when combination designs are employed that yield many different familial correlations. Model fitting—also called causal, structural, biometrical, or path modeling—gains its name because it tests the fit between a model and observed data. It is important to introduce model fitting despite the complexity of the technique, because behavioral genetic research is now nearly always reported in terms of model-fitting analyses.

If we report correlations from a study of identical twins reared apart, we implicitly have a very simple model that posits that resemblance is due solely to heredity and that lack of resemblance is due to environment. Our model can be thought of as an equation that states that the twin correlation equals heritability. The correlation for these adopted-apart identical twins represents our estimate of heritability, and the usual standard error of the correlation is the standard error of our estimate. However, we cannot test the fit of our model to the data because the model necessarily fits perfectly. Students who know algebra will recognize that we have only one equation and one unknown.

The twin method can be considered in terms of a model with two equations. One equation states that the identical twin correlation is equal to all genetic variance plus resemblance due to shared environment. The second equation equates the fraternal twin correlation to half the genetic variance plus resemblance due to shared environment. If you know how to solve simultaneous equations, you can easily show, for example, that when the two equations are solved in the case of identical and fraternal twin correlations of 0.80 and 0.50, they yield a heritability estimate of 0.60 and a shared environment estimate of 0.20. In effect, this is nothing more than doubling the difference between the correlations to estimate heritability and then saying that twin resemblance not explained by heredity is attributed to shared environmental influences. As in the previous example, we cannot test the fit of our model because the number of unknowns (two) equals the number of equations (two). Unless the model is overdetermined—that is, unless there are more equations than unknowns—we can estimate parameters but we cannot take advantage of the main benefit of model fitting, which is to test the fit of a model.

Model fitting becomes important when there are several equations and several (but fewer) unknowns. In such cases, the equations do not yield just one solution. With more complicated models, it can become difficult to set up the equations that correspond to each correlation; a technique called path analysis was developed over 60 years ago by Sewall Wright to facilitate the derivation of these equations. Path diagrams, described in Box 3.6, are frequently used to present behavioral genetic models.

Consider, for example, the combination of the twin and adoption designs, which yields correlations for four groups: adopted-apart identical and fraternal twins and identical and fraternal twins reared together. In the simplest model, the four equations are similar to those discussed previously. The twins reared together include a genetic parameter (1.0 for identical twins and 0.50 for fraternal twins) and a shared environment parameter. For twins adopted apart, the shared environment parameter is zero. This design leads to four separate estimates of genetic influence (the adopted-apart identical twin correlation, doubling the adopted-apart fraternal twin correlations, doubling the difference in correlations between identical and fraternal twins reared together, and doubling the difference in correlations between identical and fraternal twins reared apart), as well as several estimates of shared environmental

Box 3.6
Path Analysis

Over 60 years ago, Sewall Wright defined a path coefficient as the proportion of the standard deviation of one variable that is caused by variation in another variable. This path analysis has become the standard way in which models are presented in recent behavioral genetic research reports. For example, the basic behavioral genetic model is illustrated as a path diagram in Figure 3.8; the path model efficiently shows that variability in genotypes (*G*) and environments (*E*) cause variability in the phenotype (*P*) and that *G* and *E* are assumed to be uncorrelated. In fact, the path labeled *h* is the square root of heritability, because it is the proportion of the standard deviation of the phenotype that is caused by variation in the genotype. Similarly, the path *e* represents environmentally induced phenotypic variation. In other words, this path diagram illustrates the basic proposition that phenotypic variance can be due to genetic variance and to environmental variance.

Figure 3.9 is a simple path diagram for twins or siblings. P_1 refers to the score for one member of a twin pair, and P_2 refers to the other twin; as in Figure 3.8, *G* and *E* refer to genotypic and environmental variables. The correlations, r_G and r_E, refer to correlations between the twins' genotypes and environments. The model assumes that r_G is 1.0 for identical twins and 0.50 for fraternal twins. When twins are reared together, r_E is 1.0, and when they are reared apart, it is zero, in the absence of selective placement.

The main use of path analysis is to describe the components of a correlation, in this case, the correlation between phenotypes of the twins, P_1 and P_2. The path is a correlation between one variable and another in which the effects of other variables in the model have been controlled. Following certain rules,

continued

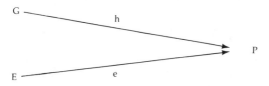

Figure 3.8. Path diagram of basic quantitative genetic model, where G is the genotype value, E is the environmental deviation, and P is the observed phenotypic value.

Box 3.6 *continued*
Path Analysis

the correlation between P_1 and P_2 can be traced through the paths connecting P_1 and P_2. The paths in a chain are multiplied. Thus, the genetic chain of paths between P_1 and P_2 are h, r_G, and h, which is the same as $h^2 r_G$. The environmental chain includes e, r_E, and e, which means that the environmental contribution to the correlation between P_1 and P_2 is $e^2 r_E$. Thus, in this path model, the correlation between P_1 and P_2 is equal to $h^2 r_G$ plus $e^2 r_E$.

From this path diagram, we can establish the equations needed for model-fitting analyses. For example, the path model indicates that the expected components underlying the correlation for identical twins reared together is:

Correlation for identical
twins reared together $= h^2 + e^2$

because both r_G and r_E are 1.0. This does not mean that the actual correlation for a particular trait is 1.0 for either genetic or environmental rea-

sons. The model merely indicates that identical twins reared together share all genetic effects that happen to affect a particular trait, and they also share all environmental effects on the trait that occur as a result of living together.

In contrast, the correlation for identical twins reared apart is equal to just h^2 because the model implies that r_E is zero in the absence of selective placement when twins are reared apart. Thus, the equations for the other twin groups are:

Correlation for identical twins
reared apart = h^2

Correlation for fraternal twins
reared together = $0.50h^2 + e^2$

Correlation for fraternal twins
reared apart = $0.50h^2$

As described in the text, model-fitting analyses can be used to test this model, compare it to alternative models, and estimate the genetic and environmental parameters and their standard errors.

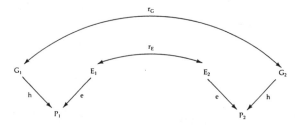

Figure 3.9. Path diagram of the resemblance between twins or siblings, where r_G is the genetic correlation and r_E is the environmental correlation.

influence. We could average these various estimates, weighting each estimate according to its sample size. However, model fitting is a much more powerful way to integrate all the information in this combination design. Model-fitting analyses can solve these four equations with two unknowns, thus providing estimates of genetic and environmental influence as well as a test of the overall fit of the model to the data. Modern analyses use what is called *maximum likelihood* estimation, which maximizes the fit between the model parameters and the observed correlations and uses more sophisticated mathematical techniques.

A major advantage of model fitting is that different models can be compared. For example, we could drop the genetic parameter from the model to determine whether the fit of the model is significantly worsened, which implies that the genetic parameter is needed to explain the data. In addition, we could test more complicated models to see whether they fit the data better than our simple model. For example, we could add a parameter that models selective placement as resemblance between reared-apart twins that is not explained by heredity. We could also add parameters that would attempt to differentiate between additive and nonadditive genetic variance. These enhanced models were tested in a recent analysis of personality data for twins reared apart and twins reared together (Plomin et al., 1988). The analyses indicated that personality is affected by nonadditive as well as additive genetic variance and that shared environment and selective placement are unimportant.

A similar path model could be used to derive expectations for the correlations for the other major combination design, the combination of family and adoption designs that yields correlations between several types of parents (biological, adoptive, and nonadoptive) and their children. A better path model, however, would incorporate both mothers and fathers and the correlation between them that represents assortative mating as well as the correlation between biological and adoptive parents that represents selective placement. We could consider each of these correlations separately and reach conclusions concerning genetic influence. For example, the correlation between biological parents and their adopted-away offspring estimates genetic influence, and we know this estimate is inflated by assortative mating and selective placement. Similarly, the correlation between adoptive parents and their adopted children estimates shared environmental influence and is also inflated by assortative mating and selective placement. In nonadoptive families, both heredity and shared environment are involved in parent-offspring resemblance, which can be increased by assortative mating. Model fitting, however, analyzes all the information simultaneously, weights each piece of information according to its sample size, tests the adequacy of the model and its assumptions, yields parameter estimates and standard errors that best fit the model, and compares alternative models.

Summary

Although it is important in an overview of behavioral genetics to mention refinements to the basic methods and more sophisticated approaches to analysis, it is also critical that we do not lose sight of the fact that adoption and twin designs are simple "natural experiments." These experiments test the extent to which familial resemblance is due to shared heredity or shared environment. Table 3.1 describes examples of the hypothetical results of family, adoption, and twin studies in their simplest form, ignoring the refinements of nonadditive genetic variance, assortative mating, selective placement, and genotype-environment correlation and interaction. Four examples are provided: (1) heritability is 0.00, shared environment is 0.25, and nonshared environment is 0.75; (2) heritability is 0.50, shared environment is 0.00, and nonshared environment is 0.50; (3) heritability is 0.50, shared environment is 0.25, and nonshared environment is 0.25; (4) heritability is 1.0.

Table 3.1 Expected correlations for family, adoption, and twin studies for four hypothetical examples of heritability and shared environment influence.

	Example 1	Example 2	Example 3	Example 4
Heritability:	0.00	0.50	0.50	1.00
Shared Environment:	0.25	0.00	0.25	0.00
Nonshared Environment:	0.75	0.50	0.25	0.00
Family Study First-degree together (0.50 G + Es)	0.25	0.25	0.50	0.50
Adoption Study First-degree adopted apart (0.50 G)	0.00	0.25	0.25	0.50
Unrelated together (Es)	0.25	0.00	0.25	0.00
Twin Study Identical together (G + Es)	0.25	0.50	0.75	1.00
Fraternal together (0.50 G + Es)	0.25	0.25	0.50	0.50

Note: G refers to genetic similarity; Es to shared environment.

In the fourth example in which heritability is 1.0, identical twins correlate 1.0, first-degree relatives correlate 0.50 regardless of whether they are reared together or apart, and genetically unrelated individuals living together correlate 0.00 because shared environment is unimportant. In the first example, heritability is zero and shared environment accounts for 25 percent of the variance. Given these conditions, first-degree relatives living together should correlate 0.25 for the behavior under study. Because heredity is unimportant, adopted-apart first-degree relatives will not resemble each other. Because shared environment accounts for 25 percent of the variance, genetically unrelated individuals living together will correlate 0.25. Correlations for twins living together will be 0.25 regardless of whether the twins are identical or fraternal.

Describing how such patterns of correlations yield estimates of heritability and shared environment was the primary goal of this chapter.

The next chapter reviews data from behavioral genetic research using the adoption and twin methods. The point of the review is that behavior rarely if ever yields results similar to example 1 in which heritability is zero or to example 4 in which heritability is 1.0. Usually, heritability is substantial but accounts for no more than half of the variance, as in examples 2 and 3. Another surprising result is that shared environment usually accounts for little variance. In other words, example 2 is most typical of results found for behavior.

Resources
Behavioral Genetic Methods

Behavioral genetic textbooks are available as resources providing greater methodological detail. These texts include *Foundations of behavior genetics* by J. L. Fuller and W. R. Thompson (St. Louis: Mosby, 1978); *Essentials of behaviour genetics* by D. A. Hay (Oxford, England: Blackwells, 1985); and *Behavioral genetics: A primer* by R. Plomin, J. C. DeFries, and G. E. McClearn (San Francisco: W. H. Freeman, 1989). The classic text on quantitative genetics, which focuses on animal breeding, is *Introduction to quantitative genetics* by D. S. Falconer (London: Longman, 1981), which is revised from the original 1960 edition.

Model Fitting

Many books are available on model fitting. An excellent text, written by a behavioral geneticist, is *Latent variable models* by J. C. Loehlin (Hillsdale, N.J.: Erlbaum, 1987). An article entitled "Comparison of the biometrical genetical, MAVA, and classical approaches to the analysis of human behavior" by J. L. Jinks and D. W. Fulker (*Psychological Bulletin*, 1970, 73:311–349) introduces model fitting to behavioral geneticists. An introduction to model fitting that employs the parent-offspring adoption model described in the text is included in *Nature and nurture during infancy and early childhood* by R. Plomin, J. C. DeFries, and D. W. Fulker (New York: Cambridge University Press, 1988).

4

How Much Does Heredity Affect Behavior?

The adoption and twin methods described in the previous chapter have been applied to the study of human behavior for the past 60 years. A mountain of data has accumulated, much of it during the past decade. Most of this research has focused on three domains: mental abilities, personality, and mental illness. The purpose of this chapter is to provide an overview of this voluminous research, emphasizing recent examples. Although a brief overview must necessarily be somewhat encyclopedic, the main point of these findings is that heredity affects many behaviors and that the answer to the question "How much does heredity affect behavior" is "a lot."

Cognitive Abilities

Throughout this chapter, issues of measurement are sidestepped in order to focus on behavioral genetic results based on widely used measures in each domain. In the domain of cognitive abilities, controversy abounds concerning the validity and the value of IQ test scores. Nonetheless, IQ tests are the most widely used measures of intelligence and also predict education and income better than any other behavioral attribute of individuals (Jensen, 1980). In this section, behavioral genetic research on IQ is described, followed by a discussion of other topics related to cognitive abilities: specific cognitive abilities, school achievement, creativity, reading disability, mental retardation, and dementias.

IQ

More behavioral genetic data have been obtained for IQ than for any other trait. Table 4.1 summarizes results from dozens of studies that include nearly one hundred thousand individuals. Adoption data show that resemblance among non-adoptive family members for IQ is due in nearly equal portions to hereditary and environmental factors. For example, the correlation between children and their "genetic-plus-environmental" parents (0.42) is approximately equal to the sum of the correlations for "genetic" parents (0.22) and "environmental" parents (0.19). Identical twins are substantially more similar in IQ scores than fraternal twins (0.86 versus 0.60). Indeed, identical twins are nearly as similar as the same persons' IQs tested twice; test-retest correlations for IQ tests are generally between 0.80 and 0.90. Even the relatively small sample of reared-apart identical twins are very similar (0.72).

Taken together, these data make it difficult to escape the conclusion that heredity significantly influences individual

Table 4.1 IQ correlations for adoption and twin studies.

	Number of Pairs	Correlation
Family Study		
First-degree		
together		
(0.50G + Es)		
Parent-offspring	8,433	0.42
Sibling	26,473	0.47
Adoption Study		
First-degree		
adopted apart		
(0.50G)		
Parent-offspring	814	0.22
Sibling	203	0.24
Unrelated		
together		
(Es)		
Adoptive parent-offspring	1,397	0.19
Adoptive sibling	714	0.32
Identical twin		
adopted apart		
(G)	65	0.72
Twin Study		
Identical		
together		
(G + Es)	4,672	0.86
Fraternal		
together		
(0.50 G + Es)	5,546	0.60

Note: G refers to genetic similarity; Es to shared environment.

Source: Bouchard & McGue, 1981, p. 1057.

differences in IQ scores. We can go beyond this issue to ask about the magnitude of the effect. How much does heredity affect IQ scores? As indicated in Chapter 3, heritability is a statistic that describes the extent to which variance for a particular characteristic is due to genetic variance among individuals in a population. Table 4.2 summarizes some heritability estimates derived from the data in Table 4.1. Doubling the difference between the correlations for identical and fraternal

Table 4.2 Summary of heritability estimates for IQ
based on data in Table 4.1.

Source of Heritability Estimate	Heritability Estimate
Doubling the difference between correlations for identical and fraternal twins reared together	0.52
Doubling the correlation for biological parents and their adopted-away offspring	0.44
Doubling the correlation for biological siblings adopted apart	0.48
Doubling the difference between correlations for nonadoptive parents and offspring and adoptive parents and adopted offspring	0.46
Doubling the difference between correlations for nonadoptive siblings and adoptive siblings	0.30
The correlation for identical twins reared apart	0.72

twins reared together produces a heritability estimate of 0.52. Doubling the correlation for parents and offspring adopted apart yields an estimate of 0.44. Doubling the correlation for siblings adopted apart provides an estimate of 0.48. Doubling the difference between the correlation for biological parents and offspring living together (0.42) and the correlation for adoptive parents and their adopted children (0.19) leads to a heritability estimate of 0.46. Doubling the difference between the correlation for biological siblings reared together (0.47) and the correlation for adoptive siblings (0.32) provides an estimate of 0.30. The small sample of identical twins reared apart yields the highest heritability estimate (0.72), although this estimate is likely to be inflated by selective placement. An ongoing study of reared-apart identical twins conducted at the University of Minnesota also yields an estimate of substantial heritability (0.69 for 48 pairs; Bouchard, 1987).

Thus, these estimates of heritability vary from about 0.30 to about 0.70. One source of this variability has recently been pointed out: direct estimates of heritability derived from the correlations for adopted-apart relatives are generally greater than indirect heritability estimates based on the difference between two correlations, such as the difference between identical and fraternal twins or the difference between nonadoptive and adoptive relatives (Plomin & Loehlin, in press). For example, in Table 4.2, the highest heritability estimate, 0.72, comes from identical twins adopted apart. The lowest correlation, 0.30, emerges for the indirect estimate based on the difference between the correlation for biological siblings and adoptive siblings. The reason for this difference is not yet known. Another unsolved source of variability in estimates of heritability for IQ scores is that older studies yield higher estimates of heritability than do more recent studies (Plomin & DeFries, 1980). In addition, as described in the previous chapter, several refinements need to be considered in providing more precise estimates of heritability, such as nonadditive genetic variance, assortative mating, and genotype-environment correlation and interaction. However, for the present purpose, it is sufficient to note that on balance, the data in Table 4.1 point to the conclusion that the heritability of IQ scores is about 0.50. This means that genetic differences among individuals account for about half of the differences in individuals' performance on IQ tests. The error surrounding this estimate may be as high as 20 percent, so we can only say with confidence that the heritability of IQ scores is between 0.30 and 0.70. Nonetheless, even if the heritability of IQ scores is at the bottom of this range, it is a remarkable finding. To explain 30 percent of the variance of anything as complex as IQ scores is an important achievement.

If half of the variance of IQ scores is due to heredity, the other half is due to environment. Much of the environmental variance appears to be of the type shared by family members. (Shared and nonshared environments were described in Chapter 3.) Genetically unrelated children adopted together yield a correlation of 0.32, suggesting that about a third of the total variance of IQ scores is due to the class of environmental influence described in the previous chapter as shared environment. The twin estimate of shared environment is similar to the direct estimate based on data for adoptive siblings. The twin study estimate of heritability is 0.52, and shared environment is the extent to which the identical twin correlation of 0.86 is not explained by heredity (that is, 0.86 − 0.52 = 0.34). Another estimate of shared environment can be derived from the difference in correlations between identical twins reared together and identical twins reared apart (0.86 − 0.72 = 0.14). However, the small sample of identical twins reared apart suggests caution in relying on this estimate. The correlation between adoptive parents and their adopted children (0.19) also suggests somewhat less shared environmental influence than the twin and sibling results. It seems reasonable that parents and their children share less similar environments than do siblings.

If about 50 percent of the variance of IQ scores is genetic in origin, and if about 30 percent of the variance is due to shared environment, the rest of the variance is due to nonshared environment (about 10 percent) and error of measurement (about 10 percent). Figure 4.1 summarizes these conclusions. Box 4.1 highlights some important developmental changes in these findings, namely, that heritability increases in magnitude during childhood and the importance of shared environmental influence declines sharply after childhood.

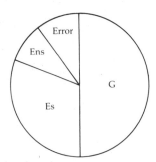

Figure 4.1. Proportions of IQ variance due to heredity (G), shared environment (Es), nonshared environment (Ens), and error of measurement.

Box 4.1
Developmental Behavioral Genetics and IQ

The results for IQ differ as a function of age. A new subdiscipline, developmental behavioral genetics, considers developmental genetic change of two types: changes in heritability and age-to-age genetic changes (Plomin, 1986). Heritability can change as different genetic and environmental systems come into play during development. Age-to-age genetic change refers to the extent to which the genes that affect a trait at one age overlap with genetic effects at another age.

In the previous discussion of behavioral genetic results for IQ, no mention was made of the age of the subjects in the various studies. How-

ever, the results for IQ differ dramatically during development, as illustrated in Figure 4.2.

Heritability increases substantially during childhood and may increase further during adolescence. Genetic effects account for about 15 percent of the variance in infant mental test scores and, by the early school years, increase in importance to about 40 percent of the variance. Increasing heritability means that the phenotypic variance of IQ scores is increasingly due to genetic differences. This may occur because more genes affect IQ scores, because early genetic effects produce increasingly larger IQ differences, or—less likely—

continued

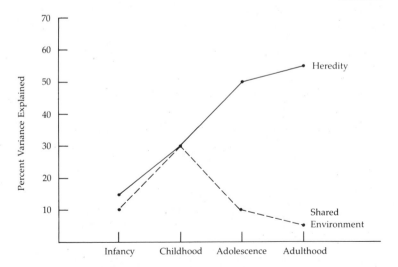

Figure 4.2. Life-span profile of genetic and shared environmental influences on IQ.

Box 4.1 *continued*
Developmental Behavioral Genetics and IQ

because environmental differences are less important. You might think that the increase in heritability is due to increasing reliability of such tests, but such is not the case. Infant and childhood tests are highly reliable, even though they do not predict later IQ.

This increase in heritability is particularly interesting. You would guess that as children develop and experience more diverse environments, environmental variance will increasingly account for phenotypic variance, which implies that heritability will thus decrease. However, this is not the case for IQ.

Heritability is not the only component of variance that changes developmentally. As shown in Figure 4.2, shared environment accounts for

about 30 percent of the variance of IQ in childhood, but its importance wanes during adolescence. This information is incorporated in Figure 4.3. Figure 4.1 showed an estimate of 30 percent shared environmental influence for IQ for two reasons: studies involving adoptive siblings took place in childhood, and twin studies overestimate shared environmental influence because twins share more experiences relevant to IQ than do nontwin siblings. For example, four recent studies of older adoptive siblings yield IQ correlations of zero on average, as compared to the average correlation of about 0.30 in studies of young adoptive siblings still living at home (Plomin, 1988). This finding suggests that although shared environmental

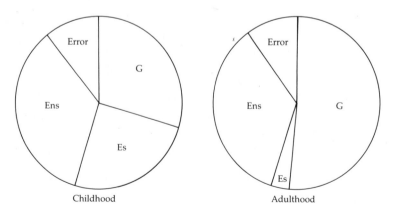

Figure 4.3. Components of IQ variance in childhood and in adulthood.

influences are important in childhood, their influence wanes to negligible levels during adolescence.

In addition to developmental changes in heritability, the second type of genetic change in development, age-to-age change and continuity, is also of importance for IQ. That is, to what extent are genetic effects at one age related to genetic effects at a later age? Genetic change means that genetic effects at one age differ from genetic effects at another age. DNA does not change—it means that genes change in their effects during development. Even though heritability is substantial for a trait in childhood and in adolescence, different genetic effects might operate at the two ages. Longitudinal data in which subjects are tested repeatedly are particularly valuable in developmental behavioral genetic research because they permit the analysis of age-to-age genetic change and continuity.

The distinction between the two types of genetic change during development is important in terms of IQ: even though heritability increases from childhood to adulthood, evidence is beginning to mount that genetic effects on IQ scores in early childhood are highly correlated with genetic effects on IQ scores in adulthood (DeFries, Plomin & LaBuda, 1987). In other words, even though the heritability of IQ is

relatively low in early childhood, genetic effects at that age continue to have an effect on individual differences in IQ in adulthood. You might wonder why phenotypic stability from childhood to adulthood is not also high for IQ. The answer is that heritability of IQ is much less than 1.0 at each age. That is, although genetic effects on IQ in childhood correlate very highly with genetic effects on IQ in adulthood, environmental effects are also important, and these effects are apparently not stable from childhood to adulthood.

How can behavioral genetic methods be used to come to this conclusion? One way is to conduct a longitudinal behavioral genetic study from childhood to adulthood. For example, if twins were studied in childhood and again in adulthood, we could first examine the heritability of IQ in childhood and in adulthood. We could also analyze the genetic contribution to IQ stability from childhood to adulthood, which indicates the extent of overlap in genetic effects at the two ages. For example, heritability of a trait could be substantial at the two ages, but the genetic correlation between the ages could be low, indicating that genetic effects at one age are different from genetic effects at the other age.

However, researchers (and, more important, research funds) do not often survive long enough to

continued

Specific Cognitive Abilities

No one believes that a single number, the IQ score, tells us all there is to know about cognitive ability. As interest in IQ as a general cognitive ability grew early in this century, researchers also drew attention to such specific cognitive factors as verbal and spatial abilities, memory, and speed of perception. Although each of these factors is itself very complex, behavioral genetic researchers study these specific cognitive abilities as a first step toward understanding the complexities of cognitive abilities. Figure 4.4 presents an example of a test used to assess spatial ability.

One of the most widely used individually administered intelligence tests is the Wechsler series, which includes tests designed for preschool children, school-age children, and adults. Relatively small twin studies (about 40 pairs of each type of twin) have been reported using each of these versions.

Box 4.1 *continued*
Developmental Behavioral Genetics and IQ

conduct longitudinal studies on people from childhood to adulthood. A new approach in developmental behavioral genetics is the use of the parent-offspring design as an "instant" longitudinal study from childhood to adulthood. If genetic changes occur during development, relatives of different ages should not be as similar as relatives of the same age. Parents and offspring are usually tested at quite different ages. Twins, however, are tested at exactly the same age. If genetic change is important during development, we would expect that twin estimates of heritability are higher than parent-offspring estimates when parents are

tested as adults and their offspring are tested as children. Methods have been developed to use such comparisons to estimate the genetic contribution to continuity from childhood to adulthood, and these methods have led to the conclusion mentioned earlier: genetic effects on IQ in childhood are highly correlated with genetic effects on IQ in adulthood. The concept of the parent-offspring design as an "instant" longitudinal study from childhood to adulthood is being put to practical use in screening infant behaviors for those that best predict adult IQ (Fulker et al., 1988).

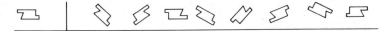

Figure 4.4. Example of a test that assesses spatial ability.

These studies suggest substantial heritability for most of the subtests—which primarily assess verbal and spatial abilities—in the preschool years (Wilson, 1975), the early school years (Segal, 1986), and adulthood (Tambs, Sundet & Magnus, 1984). Four of the Wechsler subtests (two verbal tests, a spatial test, and a perceptual speed test) were included in an adoption study that relied on the comparison between adoptive and nonadoptive family relationships, both parent-offspring and sibling comparisons (Scarr & Weinberg, 1978b). The nonadoptive correlations are higher than the adoptive correlations for all subtests, suggesting genetic influence. The only significant correlations for the adoptive relationships emerged for vocabulary, suggesting that vocabulary scores are influenced by shared environmental factors.

Although the Wechsler tests include diverse measures of cognitive abilities, they were designed to assess IQ rather than specific cognitive abilities. Specific cognitive abilities were the target of an important family study, the Hawaii Family Study of Cognition (DeFries et al., 1979). In this study, 15 tests were administered to assess verbal, spatial, perceptual speed, and memory abilities. The sample consisted of over six thousand individuals in nearly two thousand nuclear families. For both parent-offspring and sibling comparisons, familial resemblance was greater for verbal and spatial tests than for perceptual speed and memory tests. The Hawaii data also point to an issue that needs more attention: tests within each specific cognitive ability show dramatic differences in familial resemblance. For example, one spatial ability test yields one of the highest familial correlations, and another spatial ability test shows one of the lowest familial correlations. For this reason, future research on specific cognitive abilities is likely to consider more finely differentiated abilities, such as different kinds of spatial ability.

Family studies such as the Hawaii Family Study of Cognition cannot sort out the extent to which familial resemblance for specific cognitive abilities lies with nature or nurture. Although there are few adoption data on specific cognitive abilities, dozens of twin studies have been conducted. The results for three verbal tests (verbal comprehension, verbal fluency, and reasoning), a spatial test (spatial visualization), a perceptual speed test, and a memory test are summarized in Table 4.3. All of the abilities suggest heritabilities on the order of 40 percent. These results are summarized in Figure 4.5 in terms of components of variance. Compared to IQ results, specific cognitive abilities show slightly less genetic influence and slightly more shared environmental influence, especially for verbal abilities. Not enough work has been done to offer conclusions concerning developmental changes in components of variance for specific cognitive abilities.

Table 4.3 Twin correlations for tests of specific cognitive abilities.

Ability	Number of Studies	Twin Correlations	
		Identical	Fraternal
Verbal Comprehension	27	0.78	0.59
Verbal Fluency	12	0.67	0.52
Reasoning	16	0.74	0.50
Spatial Visualization	31	0.64	0.41
Perceptual Speed	15	0.70	0.47
Memory	16	0.52	0.36

Source: Nichols, 1978, p. 163.

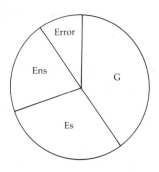

Figure 4.5. Components of variance for specific cognitive abilities.

We can conclude, as do several detailed reviews (DeFries, Vandenberg & McClearn, 1976; Plomin, 1988), that diverse cognitive tests show significant and often substantial genetic influence. However, much remains to be learned about specific cognitive abilities.

School Achievement

If heredity plays an important role in most specific cognitive abilities, it seems likely that it also affects school achievement. Several large studies of twins have employed measures of academic achievement and scholastic ability, such as tests of grammar, mathematics, and social studies.

Even report card grades show substantial genetic influence. For example, in one study, school grades were obtained for 352 pairs of identical and 668 pairs of fraternal 13-year-old twins in Sweden (Husén, 1959). The identical and fraternal twin correlations were, respectively, 0.72 and 0.57 for reading, 0.76 and 0.50 for writing, 0.81 and 0.48 for arithmetic, and 0.80 and 0.51 for history.

Twin studies of academic achievement test scores also show substantial genetic influence. For example, the largest twin study in the United States utilized data from the National Merit Scholarship Qualifying Test (Loehlin & Nichols, 1976). The twin correlations for English usage, mathematics, social studies, and natural sciences are listed in Table 4.4, and components of variance are illustrated in Figure 4.6. The results are quite similar to those for specific cognitive abilities. The average difference between the correlations for the two types of twins is about 0.20, suggesting heritabilities of about 40 percent for scholastic achievement tests.

The consistency of results with different tests is not so surprising, because the tests intercorrelate highly, about 0.60. Thinking that general cognitive ability may be responsible for this substantial intercorrelation among the tests, the researchers adjusted scores statistically to remove variance due to general scholastic ability. The residual scores nonetheless showed

Table 4.4 Twin correlations for tests of scholastic achievement.

Test	Twin Correlations Identical (1300 pairs)	Fraternal (864 pairs)
English Usage	0.72	0.52
Mathematics	0.71	0.51
Social Studies	0.69	0.52
Natural Sciences	0.64	0.45

Source: Loehlin & Nichols, 1976, p. 33.

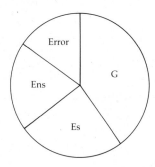

Figure 4.6. Components of variance for scholastic achievement.

greater correlations for identical twins than for fraternal twins; the difference in correlations was about 0.15. These results suggest that independent of general scholastic ability, which is related to IQ, academic achievement nonetheless shows substantial genetic influence.

Creativity

Perhaps because of conceptual and measurement problems, creativity has received less attention from behavioral geneticists than have other cognitive abilities. Creativity is usually defined in terms of the ability to think divergently rather than focusing on the single best solution to a problem. Tests of cognitive ability emphasize the latter. Tests of creativity attempt to assess such things as the ability to think of diverse uses of an object such as a brick.

In one study, 11 tests of creativity were administered to 63 identical twin pairs and 54 fraternal twin pairs from 13 to 19 years of age (Reznikoff, Domino, Bridges & Honeyman, 1973). The average identical twin correlation for the 11 tests was 0.57, and the average fraternal twin correlation was 0.44. The difference in the twin correlations suggests a heritability of about 25 percent, lower than heritability for specific cognitive abilities. Another study of creativity found even less evidence for genetic influence (Canter, 1973). Moreover, the researcher argued that there is very little genetic influence on creativity when IQ is taken into account.

A review of tests of divergent thinking yielded an average correlation of 0.61 for identical twins and 0.50 for fraternal twins in ten studies (Nichols, 1978). These twin correlations are depicted in terms of components of variance in Figure 4.7. The results are interesting because they suggest less heritability and greater influence of shared environment for creativity than for other abilities. However, more research is needed to substantiate this claim.

Reading Disability

As many as 25 percent of children have difficulty learning to read. For some, specific causes can be identified such as mental retardation, brain damage, sensory problems, and

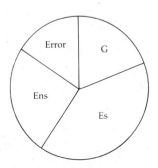

Figure 4.7. Components of variance for creativity.

cultural or educational deprivation. However, many children without such problems find it difficult to read.

Family studies have shown that reading disability runs in families. For example, a study of 1044 individuals in 125 families with a reading disabled child and 125 matched control families shows familial resemblance in that the siblings and parents of the reading disabled children performed significantly lower on reading tests than did siblings and parents of control children without reading disability (DeFries, Vogler & LaBuda, 1985). This study also shows that reading disabled children whose parents have difficulty reading are less likely to improve after a five-year period. Because this is a family study rather than an adoption study, these familial associations could be due to family environment. For example, in families with reading disabled parents, there might be minimal reinforcement and help at home for children to develop their reading skills.

Twin studies suggest that genetic factors may play an important role in familial resemblance for reading disability. There are four major twin studies: (1) a study of 97 twin pairs in which at least one twin partner was reading disabled showed 84 percent concordance (that is, both individuals were reading disabled) for identical twins and 29 percent concordance for fraternal twins (Bakwin, 1973); (2) a study of 40 pairs found 80 percent concordance for identical twins and 45 percent concordance for fraternal twins (Decker & Vandenberg, 1985); (3) a small study found evidence for genetic influence on spelling disability but not on other aspects of reading disability (Stevenson, Graham, Fredman & McLoughlin, 1987); (4) a study of 119 pairs concluded that about 30 percent of the deficit in reading is due to heritable influences (DeFries, Fulker & LaBuda, 1987).

No adoption data have as yet been reported for reading disability. A single-gene effect has been proposed for spelling disability (Smith, Kimberling, Pennington & Lubs, 1983), although subsequent analyses have not confirmed the linkage (Kimberling et al., 1985; McGuffin, 1987).

Mental Retardation

Behavioral genetic results can differ at the extremes of a distribution. For example, IQ may be strongly heritable for the entire distribution of IQ scores, but mental retardation at the low end of the IQ distribution may occur for reasons other than polygenic and "polyenvironmental" effects. Mental retardation refers to below normal intellectual capacity, and it is usually indexed by IQ scores below 70. Mild retardation involving IQs from 50 to 70 is known as familial retardation, because behavioral genetic research indicates that familial influences for this part of the IQ distribution are similar to those for the rest of the distribution, as we shall see. Research discussed later suggests that extremely low IQ scores indicating severe retardation are caused by different factors than mild mental retardation. Some causes for severe mental retardation include rare genetic factors—for example, chromosomal abnormalities such as trisomy-21 and single-gene disorders such as PKU—as well as environmental trauma such as the mother contracting German measles during pregnancy, birth complications, and nutritional deficiencies such as lack of iodine, which once frequently caused cretinism. This section begins with a description of mental retardation and chromosomal abnormalities, then considers single-gene influences, and finally discusses relevant quantitative genetic research.

Chromosomal abnormalities. Chromosomal abnormalities occur when chromosomes in the gametes do not divide properly so that some gametes receive too many or too few chromosomes. Too little genetic material is usually lethal to the embryo; however, some individuals who have too much genetic material survive. One of the single most important causes of mental retardation—about one in 1000 births—is a chromosomal abnormality in which a third chromosome appears for one of the smallest chromosomes, chromosome 21. Because chromosome 21 is one of the smallest chromosomes, having this extra DNA is not fatal to the embryo. Figure 4.8 shows the chromosomes of a woman (note the two X chromosomes) with trisomy-21.

Over a century ago, Langdon Down—who wrongly assumed that retardation was an atavism, a throwback to the early races of man—called this syndrome Mongoloid idiocy because skin at the inner corner of the eye forms a fold, making the eye look somewhat slanted. Other physical characteristics, such as a flat rather than rounded back of the head, reddish cheeks, and white spots in the iris of the eye, made these individuals a recognizable group, even though not all individuals show all of the physical features of the disorder.

Other congenital disorders such as high risk for respiratory ailments, heart malformations, and leukemia combine to reduce drastically the life span of these individuals. Down also described another syndrome he called Caucasoid idiocy, which came to be known as cretinism. The distinction was important because cretinism was shown to be environmental in origin, caused by lack of iodine, and the problem has been solved by the universal use of iodized salts. Shortly after 1956, when cell culture techniques were developed to examine chromosomes, it was shown that the vast majority of Mongolism cases involved an extra chromosome—such individuals have 47 chromosomes rather than the usual 46—and the disorder is now called trisomy-21, or Down's syndrome.

Long ago, two facts were noticed about Down's syndrome: it occurred more frequently in children born to older mothers, and behavioral genetic studies indicated that identical twins were concordant but that other relatives showed virtually no resemblance. These two facts are explained by the chromosomal origins of trisomy-21. Older mothers are more likely to produce eggs that have unequal numbers of chromosomes.

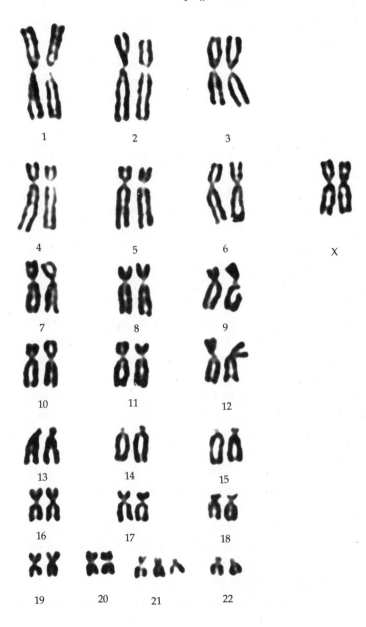

Figure 4.8. Chromosomes of a woman with trisomy-21.
(Dr. Don Fawcett/Photo Researchers Inc.)

This is thought to be due to the aging of eggs. All a woman's eggs are formed early in life, but each month an egg undergoes a last step in cell division as the woman ovulates. Concordance for trisomy-21 occurs only for identical twins, because identical twins derive from the same egg with its extra chromosome 21. There is no effective treatment for trisomy-21.

Other chromosomal abnormalities that involve missing genetic material or large amounts of extra DNA are thought to be the major source of spontaneous abortions early in pregnancy. An exception to this is the sex chromosome pair involving the large X chromosome and the small Y chromosome. When an egg with an X chromosome is fertilized by a sperm with an X chromosome, the resulting individual is female; the XY combination results in a male. Females would thus have much more genetic material than males, except that the extra X chromosome is largely inactivated in the sense that its DNA is not transcribed. For this reason, females with just one X chromosome (called Turner's syndrome) or with more than two X chromosomes, and males with more than one X chromosome (Klinefelter's syndrome), survive. Trisomy-21 and other chromosomal abnormalities are the major concerns associated with childbearing later in life, but most of these abnormalities can be detected through amniocentesis early in pregnancy. In this procedure, sloughed-off fetal cells in the amniotic fluid are obtained by means of a needle inserted through the uterine wall, and the chromosome number of these cells is determined. If a fetus is shown to have trisomy-21, parents can decide for or against abortion. It has been estimated that chromosomal abnormalities are responsible for as many as a quarter of mentally retarded individuals.

One chromosomal condition that has received attention recently is called fragile X syndrome because a certain section of the X chromosome tends to break during preparation of cell cultures and does not stain normally. The cause of this phenomenon is not known. The significance of fragile X is that it is inherited as a recessive trait on the X chromosome and appears to be a major reason for the excess of mild mental retardation in males. It has been estimated that fragile X occurs in 2 percent of males in institutionalized populations. Because females receive two X chromosomes and one of these is inactivated, females are better buffered against the effects of having one fragile X chromosome (Nussbaum & Ledbetter, 1986).

Single-gene disorders.   Phenylketonuria (PKU) is much less common than trisomy-21—about one in 10,000 births. However, it represents an important case because it is a single-gene recessive condition whose solution is environmental, not genetic, engineering. Nearly 50 years ago, it was discovered that some forms of PKU are triggered by a single recessive gene that involves the failure to metabolize the amino acid phenylalanine into tyrosine. The PKU enzyme lacks one amino acid and is unable to break down phenylalanine. As mentioned in Chapter 2, normal diets contain large amounts of phenylalanine, and this amino acid builds up and can damage the developing brain of a child, thus leading to retardation. In 1953 a diet was developed that was low in phenylalanine. Although the special diet will not improve IQ scores of older PKU individuals, it alleviates retardation when administered before six months of age until five years of age. Screening newborns for PKU is inexpensive and is now widespread in the United States; such screening has significantly reduced retardation from this cause. Formerly, PKU was responsible for about 1 percent of the population of institutionalized mentally retarded individuals but now early detection and dietary intervention has virtually eliminated PKU as a cause of severe retardation. In addition to PKU, several hundred other single-gene effects associated with mental retardation, most of them extremely rare, have been identified (McKusick, 1989).

Quantitative genetics. Although chromosomal abnormalities and single-gene defects are important sources of retardation, especially of severe retardation, most mild retardation is due to the fact that IQ scores are normally distributed. The genetic and environmental factors responsible for individual differences in IQ scores necessarily mean that many individuals will be at the low end of the distribution and thus mentally retarded. As our society becomes more complex, mild mental retardation becomes more debilitating to affected individuals. As one example of the increasing complexity of our society, the average number of years of education in the United States has doubled over the past century from six to 12 years.

Milder retardation, involving IQs from 50 to 70, is known as *familial* retardation because behavioral genetic research suggests that familial influences for this part of the IQ distribution are similar to those for the rest of the distribution. Siblings of severely retarded individuals are more likely to have normal IQs than are siblings of mildly retarded individuals, suggesting that the causes of severe retardation are not familial. In contrast, siblings of mildly retarded individuals on average tend to be mildly retarded (Johnson, Ahern & Johnson, 1976). For example, in a study of over 17,000 white children, 0.5 percent were severely retarded (IQ less than 50) and 1.2 percent were mildly retarded (IQ from 50 to 69). As shown in Figure 4.9, the severely retarded children had 20 siblings, none of whom were retarded, and who had an average IQ of 103. In contrast, the 58 siblings of the mildly retarded children included 12 retarded children; the average IQ of these siblings was only 85 (Nichols, 1984).

An important study demonstrating the familial nature of mild retardation involved 80,000 relatives of 289 mentally retarded individuals (Reed & Reed, 1965). For example, if one parent is retarded, the risk for retardation in their children is about 20 percent. If both parents are retarded, the risk is nearly 50 percent. If a sibling is also retarded, the risk is about 70

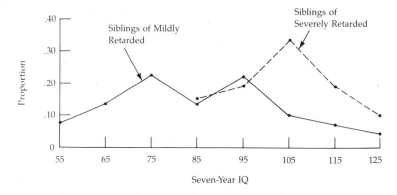

Figure 4.9. Siblings of mildy retarded children tend to be mildly retarded; siblings of severely retarded children tend to be of normal IQ. This finding suggests that mild retardation is familial but severe retardation is not (from Nichols, 1984).

percent (Anderson, 1974). Although there are no twin and adoption studies to determine the extent to which these familial influences are genetic or environmental in origin, the evidence for substantial genetic involvement in IQ scores strongly suggests that familial retardation is also, in part, influenced by heredity.

Dementias

Two diseases—Huntington's chorea and Alzheimer's disease—involve mental and motor deterioration, called dementia, similar to that which sometimes occurs with aging. However, these diseases are even more tragic because they occur earlier in life. Huntington's chorea, which affects about one in 20,000 individuals, typically begins during the 40s, with inexorable decline in mental and motor functioning, leading to death several years to several decades later. This disorder is caused by an autosomal dominant gene and yields no symptoms until most people have passed through the childbearing years—which is the reason why this lethal dominant gene can hide from natural selection. The gene for Huntington's disease has been mapped to chromosome 4. This linkage makes it possible to identify some individuals carrying the gene before they show any symptoms (Gusella et al., 1983). Mapping the gene to a place on a chromosome makes it likely that the gene for Huntington's chorea will be isolated and, eventually, that the harmful product coded by the gene will be identified.

Alzheimer's disease has been known as presenile dementia because, in its early phase, it resembles some symptoms of aging, such as impairment of memory for recent events. In a study of 30 well-documented cases of Alzheimer's disease, the risk for getting the disease was 23 percent for parents and 10 percent for siblings (Heston & Mastri, 1977). A twin study of general senility yielded concordances of 43 percent for identical twins and 8 percent for fraternal twins, suggesting genetic influence (Kallmann, 1955). A gene on chromosome 21 has been implicated in some cases of familially transmitted Alzheimer's (Goldgaber et al., 1987). However, unlike Huntington's disease, Alzheimer's is not a simple single-gene characteristic. Many identical twin pairs are discordant for Alzheimer's disease (Nee et al., 1987; Renvoize et al., 1986).

Personality

The term *personality* covers an incredible diversity of behavior. Dozens of dimensions—such as emotionality, activity level, and sociability—have been studied, each of which is likely to be as complex as intelligence. Most research on personality, especially behavioral genetic research, involves self-report questionnaires.

A landmark study involving nearly 800 pairs of adolescent twins (Loehlin & Nichols, 1976) reached two major conclusions concerning personality: a wide range of personality traits shows moderate heritability, and although environmental variance is important, virtually all of the environmental variance is of the nonshared variety. The preceding review of cognitive data led to a similar two-part conclusion: (1) nearly all cognitive abilities show genetic influence, and (2) environmental influence, after childhood, is primarily of the nonshared variety. Chapter 5 discusses the second topic at length; our focus here is on genetic influence.

Extraversion and Neuroticism

Much research has considered two "superfactors" of personality that represent major clusters of personality dimensions: extraversion and neuroticism. Extraversion encompasses such dimensions as sociability, impulsiveness, and liveliness. Neuroticism includes such dimensions as moodiness, anxiousness, and irritability. Neuroticism is a broad dimension of emotional stability-instability, not just neurotic tendencies.

A review of research involving over 25,000 pairs of twins for these two superfactors yields average heritability estimates exceeding 0.50 for both extraversion and neuroticism (Henderson, 1982). The review also points out that extraversion generally suggests evidence for nonadditive genetic variance seen in fraternal twin correlations that are lower than expected on the basis of identical twin correlations, as discussed in the previous chapter. These phenomena can be seen in examples of two recent studies. The largest twin study involves a Swedish sample of 4987 identical twin pairs and 7790 fraternal twin pairs from 17 to 49 years of age (Floderus-Myrhed, Pedersen & Rasmusson, 1980). For the entire sample, the identical and fraternal twin correlations were 0.51 and 0.21 for extraversion, respectively, and 0.50 and 0.23 for neuroticism. Another example, a study in Australia involving 2903 twin pairs, found identical and fraternal twin correlations of 0.52 and 0.17 for extraversion and 0.50 and 0.23 for neuroticism (Martin & Jardine, 1986).

Studies of first-degree relatives, however, suggest less genetic influence on personality. The average parent-offspring and sibling correlation for extraversion and neuroticism is 0.13 (Henderson, 1982). Thus, even if this familial resemblance were entirely due to heredity, heritability estimates would only be about half that suggested by the twin studies. One factor contributing to the discrepancy is likely to be nonadditive genetic variance. As discussed in Chapter 3, nonadditive genetic variance makes identical twins, but not first-degree relatives, similar. The correlations are even lower in the largest family study, conducted in Hawaii, which includes more than a thousand families (Ahern et al., 1982). The parent-offspring and sibling correlations were, respectively, −0.05 and 0.25 for extraversion and 0.17 and 0.07 for neuroticism. In this study, the offspring were assessed as adults. It is possible that parent-offspring resemblance for adult offspring and their middle-aged parents is, in fact, slight even though comparisons earlier in life suggest resemblance on the order of 0.15.

Adoption studies suggest that the familial resemblance for the two superfactors seen in family studies is indeed nearly all genetic in origin. In a review of extraversion and neuroticism data from three adoption studies, the average correlation for nonadoptive relatives was about 0.15, and the average correlation for adoptive relatives was nearly zero (Henderson, 1982). These data suggest a heritability estimate of about 0.30 for extraversion and neuroticism. However, it should be remembered that estimates based on first-degree relatives involve only additive genetic variance.

If nonadditive genetic variance is important, as suggested by the twin data, adoption studies will need to include twins in order to detect such variance. The results of a combined twin/adoption study in Sweden on middle-aged twins confirm the hypothesis that nonadditive genetic variance is important for extraversion (Pedersen, Plomin, McClearn & Friberg, 1988). In a sample of 220 identical twins reared together (MZT) and 204 fraternal twins reared together (DZT), twin correlations for extraversion are 0.54 and 0.06, which results are similar to those of other studies. The correlation for 95 pairs of identical twins reared apart (MZA) is 0.30, and the correlation for 220 pairs of fraternal twins reared apart (DZA) is 0.04. Model-fitting analyses suggest that broad heritability is about 40 percent, considering data from all four twin groups.

Correlations for neuroticism are as follows: 0.41 for MZT, 0.24 for DZT, 0.24 for MZA, and 0.28 for DZA. Although the MZT-DZT comparison and the MZA and DZA correlations suggest genetic influence, the MZA-DZA comparison does not—because the DZA correlation is as great as the MZA correlation. Nonetheless, model-fitting analyses suggest that heritability for neuroticism is about 30 percent.

In summary, two conclusions can be drawn concerning genetic influence on extraversion and neuroticism. Both traits show substantial heritability, although somewhat less than for cognitive abilities. The second conclusion is that the classical twin design yields heritability estimates that are greater than estimates from family and adoption designs. In part, this discrepancy is due to nonadditive genetic variance, especially for extraversion. As noted in Chapter 3, twin studies estimate broad heritability (which includes both additive and nonadditive genetic variance), whereas heritability estimates based on first-degree relatives primarily include additive genetic variance.

EAS Traits

As noted, extraversion and neuroticism are global traits that encompass many dimensions of personality. The core of extraversion, however, is sociability, or gregariousness, which is the extent to which individuals prefer to do things with others rather than alone. The key component of neuroticism is emotionality, the tendency to become aroused easily to fear and anger. From infancy to adulthood, these two traits and one other—activity level—have been proposed as the most heritable components of personality; this theory is referred to using the acronym EAS (that is, emotionality, activity, sociability; Buss & Plomin, 1984).

Activity level has not been studied nearly as much as has sociability and emotionality simply because activity level tends not to be included in personality questionnaires for adults. However, it is nearly always included in rating instruments for children, perhaps because of the conspicuousness of this trait in children. A review of behavioral genetic data for these three traits in infancy, childhood, adolescence, and adulthood lends support to the EAS theory (Plomin, 1986). However, it should be noted that many personality traits display genetic influence, and it is difficult to prove that some traits are more heritable than others.

One recent study of EAS traits involves the previously mentioned Swedish study of twins reared together and twins adopted apart. A unique feature of this study is that it is the only behavioral genetic study of personality in the last half of the life course—the average age of the twins was 59 years. This fact is important because heritability can change during the life course. In fact, the results of the Swedish study suggest that heritability of EAS traits is somewhat lower later in life. For example, the correlations for 90 pairs of identical twins reared apart are 0.30 for emotionality, 0.27 for activity level, and 0.20 for sociability. Model-fitting analyses that consider the results from all four groups of twins simultaneously yield heritability estimates of about 40 percent for emotionality, 25 percent for activity level, and 25 percent for sociability. Some evidence for nonadditive genetic variance was also found (Plomin et al., 1988).

Other Personality Traits

Personality research includes a wide array of other interesting traits such as rebelliousness, empathy, suspiciousness, anomie, and sensation seeking. Unlike extraversion and neuroticism or the EAS traits, these other traits have rarely been examined in more than one behavioral genetic study, and for this reason, the dozens of relevant studies are not easily summarized. However, most personality traits show some genetic influence, and evidence for nonadditive genetic variance often appears.

One recent example that also uses the powerful combination of twin and adoption designs is a study conducted in Minnesota of 44 pairs of identical twins reared apart, in addition to a small sample of fraternal twins reared apart whose average age was 36, and a large sample of identical and fraternal twins reared together (Tellegen et al., 1988). Correlations for identical twins reared apart are 0.48 for sense of well-being, 0.56 for social potency (leader who likes to be the center of attention), 0.36 for achievement (works hard, strives for mastery), 0.29 for social closeness (intimacy), 0.61 for stress reaction (neuroticism), 0.48 for alienation, 0.46 for aggression, 0.50 for control (cautious, sensible), 0.49 for harm avoidance (low risk taking), 0.53 for traditionalism (follows rules and authority), and 0.61 for absorption (imagination). These correlations—the average correlation is 0.49—are as high as those usually found for identical twins reared together. This suggests substantial heritability for some of these personality traits. Model-fitting analyses incorporating data from all four groups of twins yield an average heritability of about 0.50 for these diverse personality traits; nonadditive genetic variance appears important for about half of the traits.

As indicated previously, with few exceptions, personality traits show moderate genetic influence, at least as assessed by self-report personality questionnaires. It is generally agreed that part of the reason for this outcome involves the pervasive influence of extraversion and neuroticism in personality: because these two traits are substantially heritable, other traits related to these will also show genetic influence. Some traits independent of extraversion and neuroticism are less influenced by heredity. Two examples are traditional masculinity-femininity and tolerance for ambiguity. These traits show little genetic influence in adolescence and substantial shared environmental influence: identical and fraternal twin correlations are 0.46 and 0.40, respectively, for masculinity-femininity and 0.49 and 0.38 for tolerance of ambiguity (Loehlin, 1982). It should be noted, however, that these traits are closer to attitudes than to traditional personality traits.

In the large study of high-school twins mentioned earlier, Loehlin and Nichols (1976) included several personality questionnaires, and they concluded that identical and fraternal twin correlations for diverse measures of personality center around 0.50 and 0.30, respectively. Figure 4.10 uses these twin results to present a rough picture of the components of variance for most personality traits. These twin results estimate shared environment to be about 10 percent of the total variance. However, not surprisingly, it appears that twins share environmental influences to a greater extent than do nontwin relatives. Most notably, personality correlations for genetically unrelated individuals adopted together—a direct estimate of shared environmental variance—are about 0.05. These data suggest that shared environment accounts for only about 5 percent of the variance. This is discussed in detail in the next chapter.

Attitudes and Beliefs

Some traits involve attitudes and beliefs to a greater extent than do other personality traits. For example, in the Minnesota

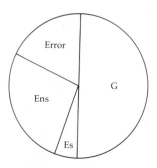

Figure 4.10. Components of variance for personality.

study, traditionalism refers to conformity and conservativeness
—the extent to which one follows rules and authority and en-
dorses traditional moral standards and strict discipline. It would
be reasonable to expect that attitudes and beliefs show less
genetic influence than personality traits such as extraversion
and neuroticism. For this reason, it has been a surprise to find
as much genetic influence for conservativeness as for other personality traits. Heritability was estimated as 0.63 for traditionalism in the Minnesota study. A review of three English
twin studies yields an average identical twin correlation of 0.67
for 894 pairs and an average fraternal twin correlation of 0.52
for 523 pairs (Eaves & Young, 1981). A recent Australian study
of 1797 identical and 1101 fraternal twin pairs yielded correlations of 0.63 and 0.46, respectively (Martin et al., 1986).

These twin correlations suggest a heritability of about 30
percent for conservatism. What is most striking about this pattern of correlations is the high fraternal twin correlation, which
could suggest substantial shared environmental effects. However, assortative mating is extremely high for this trait (spouses
correlate about 0.50), in contrast to other personality traits,
which seldom indicate significant assortative mating. Assortative mating is the reason for the large fraternal twin correlation. It also lowers the heritability estimate based on the
difference between identical and fraternal twin correlations.
When assortative mating is taken into account, heritability is
estimated to be about 50 percent (Martin et al., 1986).

Although some attitudes and beliefs such as conservatism
appear to be influenced by heredity, others are due primarily
to shared environmental influences. Religiosity, for example,
shows no genetic influence and is thus thought to be due to
environmental influence. In Loehlin and Nichols's (1976) large
study of high school twins, identical and fraternal twin correlations were 0.56 and 0.67, respectively, for belief in God, and
0.60 and 0.58 for involvement in religious affairs. Similarly, attitudes toward racial integration show no genetic influence.

Identical and fraternal twin correlations were 0.37 and 0.40, respectively. Although it is not surprising that political attitudes yield results like this, it is reassuring to find some traits that show shared environmental influence and no genetic influence. Otherwise we might have to worry about possible response biases in twin studies.

Vocational Interests

Vocational interests are related both to cognitive abilities and to personality. One of the most widely used measures of vocational interest is the Strong Vocational Interest Blank. In two twin studies—one in 1932 and the other in 1974—the average identical twin correlation was about 0.50, and the average fraternal twin correlation was about 0.25 (Carter, 1932; Roberts & Johansson, 1974). The 1974 study included over 1500 twin pairs and indicated that all of the vocational types—called realistic, intellectual, social, enterprising, conventional, and artistic—show approximately the same level of genetic influence. An adoption study also found evidence for genetic influence in comparisons between nonadoptive and adoptive parents and their children as adults (Scarr & Weinberg, 1978a).

Observational Data

It should be noted that the vast majority of behavioral genetic studies in the area of personality use self-report questionnaires. There have been several twin studies of children that have used parental ratings of their children's personality, and these studies also tend to yield results suggesting substantial genetic influence (Buss & Plomin, 1984). However, there are very few studies in which behavior is objectively observed, no doubt because of the greater expense of conducting such studies.

One observational study of infant twins suggested genetic influence on infants' social response to a stranger in their home (for example, shyness), whereas the same social behaviors directed toward the mother showed no genetic influence (Plomin & Rowe, 1979). Another observational study of school-aged children involved modeled aggression in which children were videotaped hitting an inflated clownlike plastic figure, a measure that has been shown to be valid and to relate to teacher and peer ratings of aggressiveness (Plomin, Foch & Rowe, 1981). No genetic influence was found. Twin correlations were about 0.45 for both types of twins. Observational studies of infants in the laboratory also show little evidence of genetic influence for personality traits (Goldsmith & Campos, 1986; Wilson & Matheny, 1986).

In summary, the few observational studies that have been conducted suggest much more diverse results—and less pervasive genetic influence—than do questionnaire studies. This is not simply because observational measures tend to be less reliable (Plomin, 1981); it may be because observations provide a more precise snapshot of behavior that is not averaged over many situations and across much time. The results of these observational studies promise that much remains to be learned about the genetics of personality.

Psychopathology

The two major types of psychosis (severe mental illness) have been the focus of much behavioral genetic research. One type is schizophrenia, which is characterized by long-term thought disorders, hallucinations, and disorganized speech. The second type of psychosis involves affective disorders. There are two major categories of affective disorders: depression (unipolar depression) and depression alternating with manic mood swings (bipolar depression). After a brief overview of behavioral genetic research for schizophrenia and affective disorders, other aspects of psychopathology are discussed. As indicated in Chapter 3 (Box 3.2), behavioral genetic results for psychopathology are presented in terms of concordance, which is the risk that a relative of an affected individual will also show the disorder. For example, if 100 siblings of schizophrenics were studied and ten of the siblings of these individuals were schizophrenic, the risk for siblings would be 10 percent.

Schizophrenia

Since the early part of this century, schizophrenia has been described as a major category of mental illness. The lifetime risk for schizophrenia in the general population is nearly 1 percent. In contrast, in 14 studies involving over 8000 parents of schizophrenics, 6 percent of the parents were schizophrenic. In 13 studies involving nearly 10,000 siblings of schizophrenics, the risk was 10 percent. The risk for children of schizophrenics from seven studies of over 1500 offspring of schizophrenics was 13 percent. The lower incidence among parents of schizophrenics reflects the lower fertility of schizophrenics. The average risk for first-degree relatives is 8.4 percent, more than eight times the risk for individuals chosen randomly from the population (Gottesman & Shields, 1982). However, it is important to note that over 90 percent of schizophrenics do not have schizophrenic first-degree relatives.

Twin studies indicate that this familial resemblance is due to heredity rather than shared environment. For six older studies, concordance for schizophrenia in 340 pairs of identical twins was found to be 65 percent, and fraternal twin concordance was 12 percent for 467 pairs. In five studies during the 1960s totaling 210 identical twins and 309 fraternal twins, concordances were 46 percent and 14 percent, respectively. If strict criteria are used for diagnosis of schizophrenia, the concordance rates are lower for both types of twins (Gottesman & Shields, 1982). The most recent twin study involves all male twins who are veterans of World War II (Kendler & Robinette, 1983). Twin concordances were 30.9 percent for 164 pairs of identical twins and 6.5 percent for 268 pairs of fraternal twins. This study also indicates that genetic influence on schizophrenia exceeds that for common medical conditions such as diabetes mellitus (18.8 percent concordance for identical twins versus 7.9 percent for fraternal twins), ulcers (23.8 percent versus 14.8 percent), chronic obstructive pulmonary disease (11.8 percent versus 8.2 percent), hypertension (25.9 percent versus 10.8 percent), and ischemic heart disease (29.1 percent versus 18.3 percent).

A single adoption study in 1966 by Leonard Heston turned the tide toward acceptance of genetic influence on schizophrenia. Adopted-away offspring of hospitalized chronic schizophrenic women were interviewed at the average age of 36 and compared to matched adoptees whose birth parents had no known psychopathology. Of 47 adoptees whose biological mothers were schizophrenic, five had been hospitalized for schizophrenia. None of the adoptees in the control group was schizophrenic. Studies in Denmark confirmed this finding and also found evidence for genetic influence when researchers started with schizophrenic adoptees and then searched for their adoptive and biological relatives (Rosenthal, 1972; Kety, Rosenthal, Wender & Schulsinger, 1976). These and other adoption studies of schizophrenia provide 211 first-degree biological relatives of schizophrenic adoptees and 185 control individuals (DeFries & Plomin, 1978). The incidence of schizophrenia among the biological relatives of schizophrenics is 13 percent. The incidence for the control group is 1.6 percent. The results of each study are consistent with the conclusion that schizophrenia is significantly influenced by heredity. Isolated reports of 17 pairs of adopted-apart identical twins in which at least one member of the pair was diagnosed as schizophrenic strongly support this conclusion: 11 of the 17 pairs were concordant for schizophrenia (Vandenberg, Singer & Pauls, 1986).

It is not proper to use concordance figures to draw conclusions concerning components of variance, for reasons discussed in Box 3.2. Nonetheless, some rough guesses can be made. Genetic influence should be no greater than the identical twin resemblance. It is clear that shared environmental influence is of negligible importance. For example, resemblance for reared-together relatives is no greater than resemblance for adopted-apart relatives. Also, unreliability is certainly a factor in diagnosing schizophrenia, although it is difficult to describe this error as a component of variance. A reasonable guess is that perhaps as much as 20 percent of the variance in schizophrenia may be due to diagnostic unreliability.

In Chapter 3, liability correlations were mentioned that can be calculated if we assume that a normal distribution of genetic and environmental influences underlie concordances for relatives. If these assumptions are made, correlations for the construct of liability toward schizophrenia are about 0.85 for identical twins, about 0.50 for fraternal twins, and about 0.40 for first-degree relatives. These results suggest that the heritability of the assumed construct of liability toward schizophrenia is high, perhaps in excess of 70 percent. However, it should be emphasized that this heritability refers to a hypothetical construct of an underlying liability toward schizophrenia, not the actual diagnosis of schizophrenia.

An exciting development is the discovery of a genetic marker for schizophrenia on chromosome 5 in two Icelandic families with a high incidence of schizophrenia (Sherrington et al., 1988). However, another study of a large Swedish pedigree ruled out the possibility of linkage to chromosome 5, suggesting that the chromosome 5 genetic marker may be limited to certain Icelandic families (Kennedy et al., 1988).

A final note concerning schizophrenia involves infantile autism, which shows schizophreniclike symptoms beginning early in life. However, behavioral genetic research suggests that autism is largely distinct from adult schizophrenia. For 936 parents of autistic children, about 2 percent were hospitalized for schizophrenia, as compared to the population risk of about 1 percent for schizophrenia. For 743 siblings of autistic children, only 1.7 percent were schizophrenic. Two twin studies suggest genetic influence on autism (Folstein & Rutter, 1977; Ritvo et al., 1985), and research on chromosomal abnormalities indicates that 25 percent of autistic children have the fragile X marker discussed earlier in this chapter (Gillberg & Whalstrom, 1985).

Affective Disorders

As noted earlier, there are two categories of affective disorders: unipolar depression and bipolar manic-depression. Depression—the most common form of mental illness—is marked by feelings of worthlessness, sadness, disturbances of sleep and appetite, loss of energy, and suicidal ideation; mania is characterized by hyperactivity, reduced need for sleep, and euphoria. These two types of affective disorders are referred to as unipolar depression and bipolar disorder (manic-depression). Difficulties in diagnosing affective disorders create ambiguity in ascertaining base rates in the population; one recent attempt suggests that the lifetime risk for a major depressive disorder is about 5 percent and that about 1 percent of the population has experienced both a manic and depressive episode (Robins et al., 1984). As is the case for schizophrenia, manic-depressive disorder occurs with equal frequency for males and females. Depression, however, occurs twice as frequently for females.

Affective psychoses are genetically distinct from schizophrenia. Schizophrenia occurs no more frequently in relatives of affective psychotics than in the general population, and affective psychosis occurs no more frequently than the population base rates in relatives of schizophrenics. (An in-between disorder, called "schizoaffective" disorder is generally agreed to be related to the affective disorders because family members of these individuals usually have affective disorders rather than schizophrenia.) Familial resemblance for the affective disorders is as great as for schizophrenia. In nine studies of nearly 6000 first-degree relatives of affected individuals, the risk is 9 percent (Rosenthal, 1970). Eight family studies have been published since 1975 and consistently show familial resemblance (Nurnberger & Gershon, 1981). The most recent study consisted of 235 probands with major depressive disorder and their 826 first-degree relatives (Reich et al., 1987). Major depression was diagnosed for 13 percent of the male relatives and for 30 percent of the female relatives. The familial risk for bipolar illness is lower, 5.8 percent in seven studies of 2500 first-degree relatives of bipolar probands. A recent family study of 187 families of bipolar probands reported 5.7 percent bipolar illness in 557 first-degree relatives as compared with a risk of 1.1 percent in a control sample (Rice et al., 1987). No gender difference was found for bipolar illness.

In seven studies involving a total of 146 pairs of identical twins and 278 fraternal twin pairs, the overall concordance for identical twins was 65 percent and that for fraternal twins was 14 percent, suggesting considerable genetic influence. The strict concordance of unipolar to unipolar and bipolar to bipolar is 59 percent for identical twins and 18 percent for fraternal twins (Bertelsen, 1979). For example, the largest twin study of affective disorders involved 55 pairs of identical twins and 52 pairs of fraternal twins in Denmark (Bertelsen, Harvald & Hauge, 1977). In this study, concordances were 67 and 18 percent, respectively.

These twin results for affective disorders suggest even greater genetic influence than for schizophrenia. However, unlike schizophrenia, adoption studies of affective disorders indicate far less genetic influence. Four adoption studies of affective disorders have been reported, and they yield mixed results (Loehlin, Willerman & Horn, 1988). One of the best studies, however, indicates some genetic influence (Wender et al., 1986). The biological and adoptive relatives of 71 affectively ill adoptees and 71 control adoptees were studied. Unipolar and bipolar disorders occurred in 5.2 percent of the 387 biological relatives of the probands and in 2.3 percent of the 344 biological relatives of the controls. The biological relatives of affected adoptees also showed greater rates of alcoholism (5.4 percent versus 2.0 percent) and attempted or actual suicide (7.3 percent versus 1.5 percent). The sharp differences between the twin and adoption data suggest caution in reaching conclusions about the relative importance of genetic and environmental factors. For this reason, no summary figure is included concerning components of variance for affective disorders.

An interesting recent study involves the offspring of identical twins discordant for manic-depressive illness (Bertelsen, 1985). Surprisingly, the same 10 percent risk of affective disorder was found in the offspring of identical twins, regardless of whether the identical twin was affected or not. This suggests that the identical twin who does not evidence manic-depressive illness nonetheless transmits the illness to his or her offspring to the same extent as does the ill cotwin.

Family studies suggest that depressive and manic-depressive disorders may be distinct. For example, relatives of manic-depressives have higher rates of manic-depressive disorders than do relatives of unipolar probands (Vandenberg, Singer & Pauls, 1986). Many other subtypes of affective disorders have been proposed, primarily on the basis of differential response to therapy.

In 1983 manic-depressive illness was linked to a dominant gene on the short arm of chromosome 11 in the Amish of central Pennsylvania (Egeland et al., 1987), the first time that a single major gene was unambiguously linked to psychiatric disorders. Other studies of Icelandic and non-Amish North American families, however, have shown that manic-depressive illness is *not* linked to chromosome 11 in these populations (Hodgkinson et al., 1987; Detera-Wadleigh et al., 1987). This suggests that the chromosome 11 linkage might be unique to Amish families. In addition, other studies have suggested that manic-depressive illness may be linked to the X chromosome (Baron et al., 1987).

In summary, schizophrenia and the affective disorders are genetically distinct. Both twin and adoption studies have shown that schizophrenia is influenced genetically. Although twin studies of the affective disorders suggest substantial genetic influences, for reasons not yet understood, adoption data indicate less genetic influence than the adoption studies.

High Risk Studies

Another direction in psychiatric genetics during the past twenty years is "high risk" research in which children whose biological parents were diagnosed as schizophrenic, depressed, or alcoholic are studied longitudinally. The aim of these studies is to find early indications of psychopathology, with the long-term hope of intervening to prevent the development of the disorder. It is, however, quite possible that the genes that affect adult disorders show no effects in childhood. For example, the average age of onset of schizophrenia is about 17 years, and it may be that genes involved in schizophrenia do not show their effects until late adolescence.

Fifteen long-term studies of children at risk for schizophrenia are involved in the Risk Research Consortium, which includes 1200 children with at least one schizophrenic parent and 1400 normal control subjects (Watt, Anthony, Wynne & Rolf, 1984). In early childhood, few differences are found between at-risk and control children, although by the middle childhood years, more differences emerge. Only 10 percent of the children at risk are expected to become schizophrenic, which weakens the comparison between the children at risk and the control children. The oldest children in these studies are just now entering the age of onset for schizophrenia, so that in the next few years it will be possible to determine which of the at-risk children are, in fact, schizophrenic; the earlier data for these children can then be studied in a more refined search for early indices of schizophrenia.

Over a dozen high risk studies of children of patients with depression are also underway (Orvaschel, 1983). Preliminary reports indicate results similar to those for schizophrenia: some differences can be found between at-risk and control children, but the differences are neither great nor consistent from study to study.

Other Psychopathology

Although the vast majority of research on psychopathology has focused on the most severe mental disorders called psychoses, attention has begun to turn to other milder disorders. A brief description of several areas of recent interest follow. Anxiety neurosis, sometimes known as panic disorder, shows about 20 percent risk in first-degree relatives of affected individuals, compared to only about 3 percent risk in relatives of controls (Crowe, Noyes, Pauls & Slymen, 1983). Family studies of anorexia nervosa indicate familial links with affective disorders (Gershon et al., 1984); the first twin study of anorexic twins yields concordance rates of 55 percent for 16 identical twin pairs and 7 percent for 14 fraternal twin pairs, suggesting substantial genetic influence (Holland et al., 1984). Somatization disorder, formerly known as Briquet's syndrome, involves multiple and chronic physical complaints of unknown origin, occurs primarily in females, and may be the female counterpart of antisocial behavior in males (Cloninger, Martin, Guze & Clayton, 1986). Its familial nature has been demonstrated (Guze, Cloninger, Martin & Clayton, 1986), and an adoption study indicates that adopted-away daughters of criminal and alcoholic biological fathers more often complain of multiple medical problems than a control group of female adoptees (Bohman, Cloninger, Knorring & Sigvardsson, 1984). Twin studies suggest genetic influence on antisocial personality disorder (previously called psychopathy), although this area is most often studied in terms of criminal behavior, discussed in the following section.

Delinquency and Crime

Delinquent or criminal behavior seems so much a matter of choices for which one is held accountable that most people probably never consider the possibility of genetic influence. Nonetheless, if genetic influence were to be found, it would by no means imply that criminal behavior is destined by heredity. Possible effects of genes on behavior we call criminal could include genetic influence on diverse characteristics such as body build, neurological factors, mental ability, personality, and psychopathology.

Six twin studies of juvenile delinquency yielded an 87 percent concordance for identical twins and 72 percent concordance for fraternal twins (Gottesman, Carey & Hanson, 1983). Although these results suggest some genetic influence in that identical twins are significantly more similar than fraternal twins, the most notable feature of these results is the high level of resemblance for both types of twins, suggesting substantial shared environmental influence. Rather than attempting to categorize adolescents as delinquent or not, especially when so many adolescents commit delinquent acts, one recent twin study used a continuous measure of self-reported delinquent behavior. Correlations for identical and fraternal twins were 0.71 and 0.47, respectively, again suggesting significant genetic influence and significant shared environmental influence (Rowe, 1983b). These data suggest a heritability of 48 percent and shared environmental influence of 23 percent. Further analyses of these data indicated that part of the shared environmental effect reflects the direct influence of one twin on the other—twins are often partners in crime.

The relationship between juvenile delinquency and adult criminality is not clear. Although most criminals were also delinquents, most juvenile delinquents do not become criminals. For adult criminality, evidence for genetic influence is stronger than for delinquency. It is a reasonable hypothesis that those juvenile delinquents who go on to become adult criminals may have a genetic liability.

In eight twin studies of adult criminality, the average concordances for identical and fraternal twins were 69 percent and 33 percent, respectively. The best twin study involved all male twins born on the Danish Islands from 1881 to 1910 (Christiansen, 1977). Significant and substantial genetic influence is suggested both for serious crimes against persons and for crimes against property. Identical and fraternal twin concordances are 42 percent versus 21 percent for crimes against persons and 40 percent versus 16 percent for crimes against property.

Adoption studies are consistent with the hypothesis of significant genetic influence on adult criminality. For example, one of the best studies again comes from Denmark, based on 14,427 adoptees and their biological and adoptive parents (Mednick, Gabrielli & Hutchings, 1984). For 2492 adopted sons who had neither adoptive nor biological criminal parents, 14 percent had at least one criminal conviction. For 204 adopted sons whose adoptive (but not biological) parents are criminals, 15 percent had at least one conviction. If biological (but not adoptive) parents are criminal, 20 percent (of 1226) adopted sons have criminal records; if both biological and adoptive parents are criminal, 25 percent (of 143) adopted sons were criminals. In addition, the Danish adoption study obtained data for siblings raised apart who showed 20 percent concordance, half siblings raised apart (13 percent concordance), and pairs of unrelated children reared together in the same adoptive families (9 percent concordance). Other adoption studies in Sweden and in the United States yielded similar results. Although parent-offspring adoption data suggest somewhat less genetic influence than do the twin data, all the data are consistent with a genetic hypothesis. Estimates of the magnitude of genetic influence vary so much for the twin and adoption data, however, that it is not possible to provide a summary illustration of genetic and environmental components of variance for criminality.

Alcoholism

Alcoholism runs in families: about 25 percent of the male relatives of alcoholics are themselves alcoholics, as compared with less than 5 percent of the males in the general population (Cotton, 1979). Alcoholism in a first-degree relative is by far the single best predictor of alcoholism. Twin and adoption studies have found evidence for genetic influence on the quantity of alcohol consumed among normal drinkers. For example, in a Swedish study of middle-aged twins who had been reared apart, twin correlations for total alcohol consumed per month were 0.71 for 120 pairs of identical twins reared apart and 0.31 for 290 pairs of fraternal twins reared apart (Pedersen et al., 1984). The correlations for reared-apart twins were similar to those for matched twins reared together: 0.64 and 0.27, respectively. These data suggest very substantial genetic influence and only slight influence of shared environment. However, no twin studies have focused on alcoholism per se; because the relationship between alcohol use and abuse is not understood, such studies may not apply to alcoholism. One twin study of liver cirrhosis is relevant, because advanced alcoholism is the major cause of liver cirrhosis. In a study of nearly 16,000 middle-aged male pairs of twins, concordances for liver cirrhosis were 15 percent for identical twins and 5 percent for fraternal twins (Hrubec & Omenn, 1981).

A Swedish adoption study provides the best evidence for genetic influence on alcoholism, at least in males (Bohman,

Sigvardsson & Cloninger, 1982; Cloninger, Bohman & Sigvardsson, 1981). Twenty-two percent of the adopted-away sons of biological fathers who abused alcohol were alcoholic, suggesting substantial genetic influence. Hereditary influence of biological fathers on their adopted-away sons is especially strong when the adopted-away sons are reared in lower-class adoptive families (Sigvardsson, Cloninger & Bohman, 1985). Several other smaller adoption studies are consistent with the hypothesis of genetic influence on alcoholism in males. Alcoholism appears to be much lower in females than in males, and this study suggests that genetic influence is also less for females: only 4 percent of the adopted-away daughters of alcohol-abusing biological fathers were alcoholic.

Alcohol use and abuse is a good example of how genes influence behavior. No matter how strong the hereditary propensity toward alcoholism might be for males, no one will become alcoholic unless large quantities of alcohol are consumed over long periods of time. Furthermore, it is unlikely that genes drive us to drink; what is more likely to be inherited is an absence of brakes—physiological and psychological factors that make most people want to stop drinking after a certain point of intoxication. Finding subtypes of alcoholism increases the likelihood that interventions will be found to prevent alcoholism before it irrevocably devastates the lives of affected individuals; as it is, few advanced alcoholics successfully recover.

Summary

Significant genetic influence has been found for IQ, specific cognitive abilities, school achievement, reading disability, mental retardation, numerous personality traits, attitudes, vocational interests, schizophrenia, affective disorders, delinquency, crime, and alcoholism. No longer can behavior be assumed to be unaffected by genetic influence.

Not only is genetic influence significant, it is also substantial in many cases, sometimes explaining as much as half of the variance. To appreciate the power of heredity, it should be noted that in the behavioral sciences it is rare to explain this much of the variance for any behavior. Genetic influence is so ubiquitous and pervasive in behavior that a shift in emphasis is warranted: ask not what is heritable; ask instead what is not heritable. So far, the only domain that shows little or no genetic influence involves beliefs such as religiosity and political values; another possibility is creativity independent of IQ.

This chapter has focused on one-half of the two-part message of behavioral genetics: genetic influence is significant and often substantial for nearly all behaviors examined to date. The second half of the message is just as important: the same data presented in this chapter provide the best available evidence for the importance of environmental influence. Behavioral genetics, with its balanced view that recognizes genetic as well as environmental influences, has made important contributions to our understanding of nurture, not just nature. This is the topic of the final chapter.

Resources

General References

An excellent compendium of both animal and human behavioral genetic research, including more than a thousand references, is *Foundations of behavior genetics* by John Fuller and W. R. Thompson (St. Louis: Mosby, 1978). A readable, selective review is *The roots of individuality: A survey of human behavior genetics* by L. K. Dixon and R. C. Johnson (Monterey, Calif.: Brooks/Cole, 1980). A recent review of the human behavioral genetics literature on cognitive abilities, personality, and psychopathology from a developmental perspective is *Development, genetics, and psychology* by R. Plomin (Hillsdale, N.J.: Erlbaum, 1986). A more evolutionary perspective on animal behavioral genetics can be found in *The genetics of behavior* by L. Ehrman and P. A. Parsons (Sunderland, Mass.: Sinauer Associates, 1981) and in

Behavior genetics: Principles and applications by J. L. Fuller and E. C. Simmel (Hillsdale, N.J.: Erlbaum, 1983, 1985).

The *Annual Review of Psychology* has included chapters reviewing recent developments in behavioral genetics in 1960, 1966, 1971, 1974, 1978, 1982, 1985, and 1988. *Behavior Genetics,* a bimonthly journal published since 1970, is a major repository of animal and human behavioral genetic research.

Intelligence

General discussion of research on intelligence, including a review of behavioral genetic research, can be found in *Intelligence: Heredity and environment* by P. E. Vernon (San Francisco: W. H. Freeman, 1979). Another useful resource on this topic is *Genetics, environment, and intelligence,* edited by A. Oliverio (Amsterdam: Elsevier, 1977).

Language and Learning Disabilities

Two excellent reviews in this area include an article by B. F. Pennington and S. D. Smith in *Child Development* (1983, 54:369–387) and an edited book by C. L. Ludlow and J. A. Cooper, *Genetic aspects of speech and language disorders* (New York: Academic Press, 1983).

Mental Retardation

No general review is available in this area, although the references mentioned earlier usually include mental retardation. The classic family study is *Mental retardation: A family study* by E. W. Reed and S. C. Reed (Philadelphia: Saunders, 1965).

Personality

The general references mentioned above include reviews of personality research; another review specific to personality is an article by H. H. Goldsmith in *Child Development* (1983, 54:331–355). The EAS approach to temperament is discussed more fully in *Temperament: Early developing personality traits* by A. H. Buss and R. Plomin (Hillsdale, N.J.: Erlbaum, 1984).

Psychopathology

An excellent and readable account of the genetics of schizophrenia is *Schizophrenia: The epigenetic puzzle* by I. I. Gottesman and J. Shields (Cambridge: Cambridge University Press, 1982). A general review of the major areas of psychopathology from a behavioral genetic perspective is *The heredity of behavior disorders in adults and children* by S. G. Vandenberg, S. M. Singer, and D. L. Pauls (New York: Plenum, 1986). A review of the genetics of schizophrenia, affective disorders, dementias, and alcoholism, with an emphasis on genetic counseling, is *Genes and the mind: Inheritance of mental illness* by M. T. Tsuang and R. Vandermey (Oxford: Oxford University Press, 1980).

Criminal Behavior

A general discussion concerning criminal behavior, including genetic influences, can be found in *Crime and human nature* by J. Q. Wilson and R. J. Herrnstein (New York: Simon & Schuster, 1985). Another useful reference is an edited book by S. A. Mednick, T. E. Moffitt, and S. Stack, *The causes of crime: New biological approaches* (New York: Cambridge University Press, 1987).

Alcoholism

An account of earlier behavioral genetic research on alcoholism can be found in *Is alcoholism hereditary?* by D. Goodwin (New York: Cambridge University Press, 1976). A cautionary review that emphasizes environmental in addition to genetic influences on alcoholism is presented in an article by S. Peele in *Journal of Studies on Alcohol* (1986, 47:63–73).

5

How Are Nurture and Nature Important?

Although the previous chapter focused on what is known about genetic influence on behavior, behavioral genetics has two messages: nature *and* nurture. One message, the point of the previous chapter, is that for most behaviors studied so far, genetic influence is significant and substantial. The other message is that the same behavioral genetic data yield the strongest available evidence for the importance of environmental influence.

Not only does genetic research document the great importance of environmental influence in behavioral development, it also provides novel tools to explore environmental influence—methods that address the potential importance of both nature and nurture. The major theme of this chapter is that explorations of environmental influence are enhanced by also considering heredity. When we review social and behavioral research at the turn of the century, we will find that behavioral genetic research has revealed as much about the environment as about heredity.

The first two sections of this chapter review the data presented in Chapter 4 in relation to nurture rather than nature. First, we emphasize the importance of environmental variance. The second section discusses one of the most important findings in behavioral genetics: nonshared environment. That is, environmental variance works in a way very different from how the environment was thought to work. Contrary to what we might have believed, the environment primarily operates to make children growing up in the same family different from, rather than similar to, one another. Because these environmental influences do not produce resemblance between family members, they are referred to as *nonshared environment.*

The third section of this chapter raises a new topic of research in behavioral genetics. Recent research has discovered genetic influence on measures of the family environment, as well as genetic mediation of associations between environmental measures and measures of behavioral development. The major point of this final section is that environmental influences in the family need to be studied using methods that recognize hereditary resemblance among family members.

The Importance of Environment

Demonstration of significant genetic influence for many behaviors does not imply that heredity alone is responsible for behavioral differences among individuals. Research described in the previous chapter suggests that heritability of many behaviors are in the range of 30 percent (beliefs, schizophrenia), 40 percent (specific cognitive abilities, personality, delinquency), and occasionally 50 percent (IQ). This means that one-third to one-half of the variance for most behaviors is due to genetic differences among individuals. These same results thus indicate that the majority of the variance for most behaviors is due to nongenetic factors, the environment. In other words, the major reason why one person is diagnosed as schizophrenic and another is not has to do with environmental factors.

This conclusion emerges from twin and adoption analyses of genetic and environmental components of variance. One piece in the puzzle makes the point most clearly. To the extent that identical twins are different, environment must be important. For example, the concordance for schizophrenia for identical twins is about 40 percent. The fact that identical twins are much more similar than expected on the basis of the population incidence of 1 percent for schizophrenia indicates genetic influence. This was the point emphasized in Chapter 4. However, the fact that they are much less similar than 100 percent concordance provides strong evidence for an important role for nongenetic factors. There is no way to explain differences within pairs of identical twins in terms of genetics, because members of identical twin pairs are genetically identical to each other.

In behavioral genetic research, the word *environment* includes any nonhereditary influence, such as biological factors— for example, physical trauma, nutritional factors, and even DNA itself. For instance, individual differences in the common forms of cancer show little hereditary influence. Identical twins show only 6 percent concordance for breast cancer, only 2 percent concordance for colon cancer, and only 2 percent concordance for rectal cancer. The corresponding fraternal twin concordances are 5 percent, 3 percent, and 0 percent (Holm, Hauge & Jensen, 1982). Nonetheless, DNA is thought to be importantly involved in the failure of mechanisms to control the rapid cell growth that leads to cancer, perhaps because of viral infections that take over the genetic control of cells.

Of course, although biological events can induce environmental variation, environmental variation can also be brought about by the psychosocial environmental factors that tend to be the focus of attention in the social and behavioral sciences. These include such environmental influences on the child as interactions with parents and siblings; with teachers, classmates, and friends; and with books, music, and television. Specific associations between such environmental factors and children's development are discussed later in this chapter.

This section is brief because its point is simple: behavioral genetic data provide the best available evidence for the importance of environmental variation. Although simple, this point is profoundly important for the future of social and behavioral science.

Nonshared and Shared Environmental Influence

One striking fact that stands out in the previous chapter is that children growing up in the same family do not usually resemble each other unless they are genetically related. These results suggest that most environmental variance relevant to behavioral development is not shared by family members. Just as total phenotypic variation can be divided into components of variance due to genetic and nongenetic influences, the environmental component of variance can be divided into two components. One component is shared by family members, and this makes them resemble each other environmentally. The second component of environmental variance is not shared.

The distinction between shared and nonshared environmental variance has existed implicitly at least since the beginning of behavioral genetics. The goal of behavioral genetic methods has been to identify the extent to which familial resemblance is due to heredity or to shared environmental influence. Only during the past decade has the importance of nonshared environmental influence been fully appreciated. Shared environmental influence has been called E_2, between-family, and common environmental variance. Labels that have been used to refer to nonshared environment include E_1, within-family, individual, unique, and specific environmental variance.

Before we take up the topic of what these nonshared environmental factors might be, in the next section we will review the evidence for the importance of nonshared environment.

In order to understand better the distinction between shared and nonshared factors, consider parental treatment. We have assumed that parents in some families are, say, permissive and parents in other families are authoritarian. In the past, researchers have examined the effects of permissive/authoritarian parenting by correlating the environmental measure across families with children's developmental outcomes such as their adjustment. This approach, which reflects the vast majority of research on environmental influences, studies only one child per family because it is implicitly assumed that other children in the family of authoritarian parents would also experience authoritarian parenting. That is, the assumption is made that permissive/authoritarian parenting is shared by two children growing up in the same family. This is not the case. To the extent that parenting styles are shared by two children in the same family, these styles *cannot* be important in development. What is important are environmental factors that are not shared by children in the same family. In the case of permissive/authoritarian parenting, what might be important is that one child is treated more permissively than another in the same family. The way to find out what factors contribute to nonshared environment is to study more than one child per family. We can then ask what makes two children in the same family so different from each other.

Evidence for the Importance
of Nonshared Environment

Resemblance between genetically unrelated individuals who are adopted together directly assesses the shared environmental component of variance. As explained in Chapter 4, their correlation indicates the total impact of all shared environmental factors that make individuals growing up in the same family similar to one another. Because correlations for adoptive siblings are so small for personality and psychopathology (and for IQ after childhood), this implies that the shared environment component of variance is negligible. Because environmental variation is important, usually accounting for half of the variance for most domains of behavior, this in turn implies that most of the environmental variance is of the nonshared variety.

Behavioral genetic designs other than the study of adoptive siblings yield similarly low estimates of shared environmental influence and correspondingly high estimates of nonshared environmental influence. For example, differences within pairs of identical twins can only be caused by nongenetic factors. Thus, the extent to which the identical twin correlation is less than 1.0 is due to nonshared environment and error of measurement. (Error of measurement also makes family members, including identical twins, appear different, because measurement errors do not correlate for family members. The portion of variance due to unreliability of measurement needs to be considered in interpreting nonshared environmental influence.) The classical twin design, which compares resemblance of identical and fraternal twins reared together, estimates shared environmental influence as the extent to which twin resemblance cannot be explained by hereditary similarity.

Consider the results for most measures of personality, as illustrated in Figure 4.10 in the previous chapter. Correlations for adoptive siblings or for adoptive parents and their adopted offspring are about 0.05, suggesting that shared environmental influence accounts for only about 5 percent of the variance.

Studies of first-degree relatives living together yield correlations of about 0.20, whereas correlations for adopted-apart relatives tend to be about 0.15, suggesting again that shared environment accounts for about 5 percent of the variance (that is, 0.20 − 0.15). Correlations for identical and fraternal twins are about 0.50 and 0.30, respectively, suggesting heritabilities of about 40 percent. Because the identical twin correlation is 0.50 and the proportion of variance due to heredity is 0.40, shared environment is estimated to be about 10 percent. That is, in the classical twin design, shared environment is estimated as the extent to which identical twin resemblance cannot be explained by hereditary similarity. Heredity contributes 0.40 to their phenotypic correlation of 0.50, and the rest of their resemblance is due to shared environment. This shared environment estimate of about 10 percent may be higher than the previous estimates because twins share more experiences in common than do nontwin relatives.

These data indicate that although family members resemble each other, this resemblance is primarily due to heredity rather than to shared environmental influences. As illustrated in Figure 4.10, behavioral genetic studies of personality generally yield heritability estimates of about 40 percent. Thus, nongenetic influence accounts for about 60 percent of the variance. As noted earlier, some of this nongenetic variance may be due to error of measurement. Variance due to error of measurement can be assessed by estimating the reliability of the measure. For example, the measure may be assessed twice for the same individuals. The test-retest correlation is a conservative estimate of the extent to which a measure is reliable. Self-report personality questionnaires show test-retest correlations of about 0.80, which means that about 80 percent of the variance is reliable and that about 20 percent of the variance is not reliable. This unreliable variance is included in the nongenetic component of variance. The amount of reliable environmental variance is about 40 percent (60 percent − 20 percent). Of this reliable environmental variance, only about 5 percent is due to shared environment, and the rest represents nonshared environmental influence.

In other words, the data from various adoption and twin studies point to the conclusion that environmental variation is important but that most of this environmental variation is of the nonshared variety. This picture will no doubt change as more is learned about particular personality traits and the effects of differences during the life course. However, it is remarkable how the results for very diverse personality traits tend to lead to this conclusion. The only exceptions that show shared environmental influence are a few attitude/personality traits, such as traditional masculinity/femininity and tolerance of ambiguity, and religious and political beliefs.

Similar results indicating the importance of nonshared environment are seen for adult IQ, as shown in Figure 4.3. The story about IQ is particularly interesting because it includes a developmental twist. Shared environmental influences are important in childhood, accounting for perhaps 30 percent of the total variance in IQ scores. For example, the average correlation for pairs of unrelated children adopted together is 0.32. An interesting study of 50 pairs of genetically unrelated children 8 to 13 years of age who were reared together on kibbutzim in Israel yielded a correlation of 0.29 for IQ (Nathan & Guttman, 1984). However, by the time children become adolescents and leave their families, shared environmental influence drops to negligible levels. As indicated in the research described in Chapter 4, after childhood nearly all environmental variance that affects IQ scores is of the nonshared variety.

The results for specific cognitive abilities, shown in Figure 4.5, suggest that about 25 percent of the variance may be due to shared environmental influence. However, not enough work has been done to know whether specific cognitive abilities, like IQ, show a decline in the importance of shared environmental influence after childhood.

It is interesting that shared environmental influence appears to be greater for verbal abilities than for other specific cognitive abilities. Measures of school achievement show somewhat more influence of shared environment than do specific cognitive abilities, at least in high school students and in twin studies (Figure 4.6). However, we need to keep in mind that twin studies probably overestimate shared environmental influences, because twins share more similar experiences than do nontwin relatives. Nonetheless, nearly a quarter of the reliable variance for school achievement measures is due to nonshared environmental factors. Tests of creativity (Figure 4.7) suggest less genetic influence and more shared environmental influence than other measures in the cognitive domain.

As discussed in Chapter 4, behavioral genetic results for other domains of behavior also indicate the importance of nonshared environment. For example, for psychopathology, nearly all environmental influence is of the nonshared variety. Twin studies suggest greater shared environmental variance for delinquency than for traits in the domains of personality and psychopathology; it is likely that twins are partners in crime. For criminality and alcoholism, shared environmental influence also appears to be minimal.

What Are Nonshared Environmental Influences?

The importance of nonshared environment is one of the most significant behavioral genetic discoveries. It implies that the environment shared by children growing up in the same family does not make children similar to one another. For example, genetically related individuals adopted away from a schizophrenic proband are just as likely to become schizophrenic as are individuals reared in the same family with the schizophrenic proband. This means that shared environmental factors, the sort studied in the vast majority of environmental research, are not important in development.

In addition, this finding suggests a new way of thinking about environmental influences. In the past, it usually has been assumed that environmental influence operates on a family-by-family basis. That is, many environmental factors differ

across families, such as socioeconomic status, parental education, and parental childrearing attitudes and practices. Such
between-family environmental influences have been the focus
of previous research. However, shared environmental factors
that do not differ between children growing up in the same
family do not influence behavioral development. The important question becomes "Why are children in the same family
so different from one another?" and the practical key to unlock
this riddle is to study more than one child per family. Only
by studying more than one child per family can we identify
experiences that differ between children in a family and then
relate these experiential differences to siblings' behavior.

An important issue for future research is to begin to identify the nonshared environmental influences that are so important in development. These influences need not be
mysterious. Any environmental factor that has been studied
in the traditional family-by-family approach can be recon-
sidered in terms of experiential differences within a family. One
restriction is that the measure must be specific to each child.
That is, many of our measures of the family environment are
general, such as a family's socioeconomic status. The search
for nonshared environment requires that we measure environmental factors specific to the individual child. Even
socioeconomic status could be studied in this way. For example, socioeconomic status changes during the life course of the
family. These relatively small changes in the family's fortune
could make a big difference in the outcomes for children, who
experience the financial ups and downs at different points in
their development.

Other environmental factors are more easily thought about
in terms of nonshared environment. For example, differential
parental behavior toward children in the same family could
have an important impact in creating differences among the
children. The folksinger/comedian brothers popular in the
1960s, the Smothers Brothers, had a running joke that "Mom

always loved you best." Such small differences in parental treatment within the family might have a large effect on differences in each child's development. Similarly, the behavior of siblings toward each other—as well as aspects of their relationship such as rivalry, closeness, and supportiveness—could be an important source of differential experience for children in the same family. Another set of variables related to siblings' nonshared experiences involves family composition, such as birth order and gender differences. Finally, experiences outside the family could also play a role in creating behavioral differences for children in the same family—for example, siblings in the same family often have nonoverlapping peer groups at school and different friends outside of school. These are systematic sources of nonshared environment. It is also possible that nonsystematic factors, such as accidents and illnesses or other idiosyncratic experiences, initiate differences among siblings that when compounded over time make children in the same family different in unpredictable ways.

Behavioral geneticists have begun to work with environmental researchers in the exciting new area of nonshared environment in order to identify specific nonshared environmental factors. The key to this research is to ask what makes children in the same family so different from one another and to study more than one child per family in order to answer the question. Three steps are involved: (1) identify experiences that are not shared by children in the same family, (2) relate differences in the experiences of children in the same family to their behavioral outcomes, and (3) determine the causal direction of associations between experiential differences and behavioral outcomes.

Concerning the third point, it is possible that sibling differences in experience reflect rather than affect differences in behavior. For example, suppose that differences in parental affection are associated with siblings' sociability. It is possible that genetically influenced differences in siblings' sociability might lead parents to respond differently to their children. Behavioral genetic methods are useful in addressing this third issue. One approach is to relate behavioral differences within pairs of identical twins to their experiential differences, because members of identical twin pairs do not differ genetically. Another approach is to compare adoptive and nonadoptive siblings.

Several studies in which young siblings were observed in their homes have been conducted. These studies indicate that siblings do, in fact, experience quite different family environments. Much of the research to date, however, involves siblings' perceptions of their experiences. Even if children in the same family appear to receive the same environmental treatment during home observations, this does not mean that they experienced the treatment similarly. A self-report instrument has been developed called the Sibling Inventory of Differential Experience (SIDE; Daniels & Plomin, 1985). The SIDE asks each sibling to compare his experiences to those of another sibling in the domains of parental treatment, sibling interaction, peer characteristics, and events specific to the individual. Research with the SIDE indicates that siblings perceive that their parents treat them quite similarly, and other research suggests that parents themselves perceive that they treat their children similarly (Daniels, Dunn, Furstenberg & Plomin, 1985). Nonetheless, as mentioned earlier, it is possible that small differences in parental treatment lead to large differences in development. Research with the SIDE also indicates that siblings perceive their experiences to differ more in interactions with each other and with peers than with their parents. Other studies, including observational research, add to the conclusion that siblings in the same family experience different environments, perhaps with respect to parental treatment and probably in their interaction with each other and with their peers.

These studies also show that sibling differences in experiences, especially perceived experiences, relate to differences in siblings' developmental outcomes. For example, this research suggests that the sibling who feels closer to her mother (and whose mother reports feeling closer to her) is better adjusted psychologically. However, much remains to be learned about experiences that are not shared by children in the same family and the association of these experiences with developmental outcomes.

Some progress has also been made in the third step of the research program: assessing the extent to which such associations are mediated genetically. That is, it is tempting to interpret such associations causally in the following way: the sibling to whom the mother is closer is better adjusted *because* of the mother's closeness. However, it is possible that the causal direction is the other way around. Sibling differences in experience might reflect genetically influenced differences in behavior. For example, if psychological adjustment is influenced genetically, siblings will differ in adjustment for genetic reasons. Differences in a mother's closeness to her two children might occur because she finds it difficult to feel as close to the child who is less well adjusted.

Associations between nonshared environment and children's outcomes are not likely to be mediated genetically, because measures of nonshared environment appear to show little genetic influence. For example, in a study of 174 biological siblings and 222 adoptive siblings, the average sibling differences on the SIDE were of the same magnitude for biological siblings (0.69) and adoptive siblings (0.76), suggesting little genetic influence on the SIDE (Daniels & Plomin, 1985). If genetic influences were important on the SIDE measure, we would expect genetically related siblings to show smaller differences (greater resemblance) for the SIDE scores than do adoptive siblings. Moreover, associations between the SIDE and personality do not appear to be mediated genetically in that the associations are just as strong for adoptive and nonadoptive siblings (Daniels, 1987).

Single-child families.   One question that often arises in the relevance of nonshared environment to the study of singletons, children in single-child families. Because over 80 percent of the families in the United States have more than one child, it is important to understand why children in a family are so different even if nonshared environmental influences found in studies of siblings do not generalize to singletons. However, it is likely that the search for causes of sibling differences will also yield clues to environmental factors important for singletons. This is because such research will provide heightened sensitivity to subtle nuances of children's experiences that show up in differential experiences of two children in the same family. The important point in relation to the search for nonshared environmental influence is the obvious one that the study of singletons cannot isolate factors that make two children in the same family different from one another. Because this is the best clue we have as to the identification of environmental influences relevant to psychological development, it makes sense to focus on environmental sources of differences between children in the same family and then to explore the relevance of such environmental factors to singletons.

Conclusions concerning nonshared environment.   In summary, research to date on nonshared environment leads to several conclusions:

1. Behavioral genetic studies consistently point to nonshared environment as the most important source of environmental variance for personality and psychopathology and for IQ after childhood.
2. When more than one child is studied per family, it is apparent that siblings in the same family experience considerably different environments in terms of their treatment of each other, their peer interactions, and, perhaps, parental treatment.

3. Family constellation variables such as birth order and gender differences account for a small (1 to 5 percent) portion of the variance of developmental outcomes.
4. Differences in siblings' experiences relate significantly to siblings' differences in behavior, implying that nonshared environmental influences are at least, in part, systematic.
5. Measures of nonshared environment do not primarily reflect genetic differences between children in the same family.

Although the first few steps have been taken in identifying specific sources of nonshared environment, much remains to be learned. A crucial question is whether most nonshared environmental variation is systematic. Many other questions are also important: Which specific nonshared environmental factors account for most variance in behavioral outcomes? Which sibling differences in behavior are most strongly related to specific nonshared influences? How do such behavior-environment associations change developmentally? The broad question "Why are children in the same family so different from one another?" is likely to lead to different answers for different domains of behavior and for different phases of the life course. However, the answers that emerge are not only answers to the question about sibling differences but have an importance that is far more general: these answers will greatly advance our understanding of the environmental origins of individual differences in development.

The Nature of Nurture

In addition to demonstrating the importance of environmental variance and, more specifically, of nonshared environment, behavioral genetic research has made important advances in understanding the interface between nature and nurture. Recent research has shown that heredity can affect environmental measures and that heredity can also mediate associations between measures of the environment and behavioral outcomes. This is an important finding because it means that some supposedly environmental factors that influence development are in fact genetic factors. For example, suppose that parents who read more to their children have brighter children. On the basis of such a finding one might want to suggest that all parents read more to their children in the hope of making all children brighter. However, heredity might be involved in the extent to which parents read to children because brighter parents read more to their children, because brighter children elicit more reading from their parents, or both. If genetic factors are responsible for the association between reading and children's IQ, caution is warranted for the proposed intervention that all parents should read more to their children in order to increase their children's IQ.

This is not to say that finding genetic effects on environmental measures necessarily disqualifies attempts to intervene. As is the case for all behavioral genetic analyses, heritability only indicates that genetic factors are important given the current range of genetic and environmental influences. It may be, for example, that most of the reason why some parents read more to their children depends on genetic factors in the parent or child or both. Nonetheless, it is possible that most children would profit if their parents were to read to them more often. In addition, parents' reading to a child may be particularly important for certain children, such as lower-IQ children. An intervention targeted toward such groups may be effective even if the intervention does not affect all children.

Genetic Influence on Environmental Measures

The possibility of genetic influence on measures of the environment is not as paradoxical as it seems once you realize that measures of environment are often indirect measures of behavior. For example, two frequently studied dimensions of the family environment are parental love and control. These measures are obviously measures of parental behavior. For example, some parents hug and kiss their children whenever they are within reach. Others rarely display physical affection. Some parents are firm disciplinarians, and others avoid disciplining their children. Parental behavior is also ultimately responsible for the physical features of the family environment. For example, the most widely used environmental item in studies of mental development is the number of books in the home. But books do not magically appear on the shelves—parents usually put them there.

Given that measures of the home environment indirectly assess parental behavior, these environmental measures can be used in behavioral genetic studies in the same way as any other phenotypic measure. Research on the genetics of environmental measures will be reviewed shortly. However, it should come as no surprise that behavioral genetic studies of environmental measures show genetic influence because behavioral genetic research has shown that variability for most behaviors shows some genetic influence. Before presenting this research, let us consider in greater detail how genetics can affect measures of environment and how we can assess these effects.

How can heredity affect measures of the environment?
Genetic influence can affect measures of family environment in two ways. First, genetically influenced characteristics of parents, such as parents' cognitive abilities and personality, can affect ratings on measures of the family environment. Number of books in the home, for example, could show genetic influence because brighter people read more. Second, parents can respond to genetically influenced characteristics of their children such as personality, abilities, and physique. In the example used earlier, the frequency with which parents read to

their children could be governed by genetic characteristics of the children. For instance, brighter children might get their parents to read to them more often.

How can we assess genetic influence on measures of family environment?   Any behavioral genetic research design can help us do this. If measures of parenting are influenced by genetic differences among parents and children, identical twins who are parents should be more similar in their parenting than are fraternal twin parents. In addition, identical twin children should be treated more similarly than fraternal twins, and nonadoptive siblings should be treated more similarly than adoptive siblings. Studies of twin parents represent the most direct approach to the issue. However, studies in this area are primarily limited to studies of children, including their perceptions of their family environment and observational studies of their parents' interaction with them.

Research on genetic influence on environmental measures.   The first studies of genetic influence on environmental measures were twin studies that analyzed adolescent twins' perceptions of their family environment (Rowe, 1981; 1983a). Twins were asked to rate the affectionateness and control of their parents in two separate studies of adolescent twins using different measures of the family environment. Affectionateness refers not only to physical affection but also to the parents' general warmth and supportiveness to the child. Control involves the parents' attempts to set and enforce rules and to organize the child's life. The fascinating finding was that identical twin correlations were significantly greater than fraternal twin correlations for measures of parental warmth (affection, acceptance) but not for measures of parental control. In other words, genetic factors affect the adolescents' perceptions of their parents' warmth but not of control. This could occur because adolescents' perceptions of their parents' affection reflect genetic differences in the adolescents' personality and adjustment. For example, more anxious adolescents might be sensitive to imagined slights or rebuffs from their parents. Another possibility is that adolescents' perceptions are accurate and their parents' affection is related to genetically influenced characteristics of the adolescents, such as sociability.

Similar results have been found in a study of elderly twins in Sweden who were asked about their perceptions of their childhood family environment, as viewed half a century later (Plomin et al., 1988). This study combines the classical twin study that compares identical and fraternal twins reared together with the adoption design of identical and fraternal twins reared apart. The sample includes over 300 pairs of twins reared apart and a matched sample of twins reared together. Despite the procedural differences between this study and Rowe's two studies of adolescents, the results are similar. Perceptions of control show little genetic influence, whereas other aspects of the family environment show genetic influence. For example, a warmth-related dimension labeled "cohesiveness" yielded the highest correlation of eight scales for identical twins reared apart (0.41), and the lowest correlation (−0.03) was observed for a scale called "control." In fact, it appears that all scales except control show significant genetic influence. Model-fitting analyses using the data from reared-apart and reared-together identical and fraternal twins confirm genetic influence on all dimensions of the family environment except control. The correlations for identical twins reared apart from early in life are particularly impressive because these individuals were reared in different families. This could mean that genetic influence is in the eye of the beholder—that is, heredity may be involved in subjective characteristics that affect perceptions of the family environment. However, it is also possible that members of the two families responded similarly to genetically influenced characteristics of the separated identical twins.

Research of this type, using adoption designs and young children, also implicates genetic influence. In the Colorado Adoption Project, for example, home environments of non-adoptive and adoptive siblings are assessed yearly during childhood, and measures of environment are made objectively rather than relying on children's perceptions (Plomin, DeFries & Fulker, 1988). One measure employed in the study is the Home Observation for Measurement of the Environment (HOME; Caldwell & Bradley, 1978). The HOME is one of the most widely used measures of the home environment relevant to cognitive development. HOME correlations for nonadoptive siblings are greater than for adoptive siblings. At 12 months, the nonadoptive and adoptive sibling correlations are 0.50 and 0.36, respectively. At two years, the correlations are 0.50 and 0.32. The fact that the correlations for nonadoptive siblings are greater than correlations for adoptive siblings suggests that parental behavior, as assessed by the HOME, in part reflects genetic differences among children. The fact that the correlations for adoptive siblings are significant indicates, not surprisingly, that the HOME also assesses environmental influences shared by siblings. The surprise is that genetic influence should count for so much in this objective measure of the home environment.

Another set of studies on this sample adds videotaped observational data. Ratings were made of videotapes of mothers interacting with each of two adoptive or nonadoptive siblings when each child was one, two, and three years old (Dunn & Plomin, 1986). One benefit of this approach, unlike the HOME and many other measures of the family environment, is that maternal behavior specific to each child can be assessed. This research also indicates that mothers behave more similarly to their children if they are biological rather than adoptive siblings. Moreover, this evidence for genetic influence again emerged for maternal affection, not for maternal control.

In summary, these first analyses of genetic influence on environmental measures suggest that some of the variance on environmental measures may reflect differences that are genetic in origin. These measures include children's perceptions of parental treatment as well as more objective measures such as the HOME and ratings of videotaped observations of mother-child interaction. The importance of this finding is that measures of the environment are not necessarily environmental. Heredity can play a role in such measures via genetically influenced characteristics of parents and children. As mentioned earlier, this finding has implications for intervention.

Several directions for future research are also suggested by these findings. Which environmental measures are most and least influenced genetically? All we know so far is that measures of parental control show little genetic influence, whereas other dimensions of parental behavior show significant genetic influence. Are genetic influences on self-reported perceptions of the family environment in the eye of the beholder, or do these perceptions accurately reflect genetically influenced characteristics of family members? What are the processes by which heredity affects measures of family environment?

As interesting as it is to consider genetic influence on environmental measures, the real importance of this topic lies in the possibility that genetic influences on environmental measures are translated into genetic effects on the relationship between environmental measures and children's development. This is the topic of the next section.

Genetic Influence on
Environment-Development Associations

The previous section focused on measurement of the environment alone. In contrast, we now consider the association between measures of the environment and measures of children's development and possible genetic influence on this association. The example used earlier involved the association between parents' reading to children and the children's IQ. We noted that this association could be mediated genetically if, for example, brighter parents read more often to their children or if brighter children elicit more reading from their parents. An empirical example concerns the HOME, which shows genetic influence, as indicated in the previous section. The HOME correlates with children's IQ, and we can ask whether genetic factors mediate the association between the HOME and children's IQ. Obviously, the family environment does not have DNA and cannot be inherited. However, the point is that measures of the family environment can tap genetically influenced characteristics of parents and of children.

Assessing genetic influence on environment-development associations.   The path diagram in Figure 5.1 may help illustrate possible genetic involvement in associations between environmental measures and children's development. In adoptive families, an environmental measure or index (I) is associated with the environment of children (E_c) and affects children's behavior (P_c) solely for environmental reasons. This is the way environmental measures have traditionally been considered—

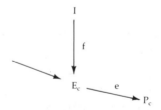

Figure 5.1. Path diagram illustrating the association between a measure of the family environment (I) and a measure of children's development (P_c) in adoptive families in which parents and children do not share heredity. (Adapted from Plomin, Loehlin & DeFries, 1985. Used with permission.)

without including the possible effects of genetic relatedness of parents and offspring. In adoptive families, parents and their children do not share heredity. In nonadoptive families, however, parents share heredity as well as environment with their children, and it is possible that hereditary similarity between parents and children is responsible for associations between environmental measures and developmental outcomes.

This possibility is indicated in the path diagram in Figure 5.2. That is, in adoptive families, the association between I and P_c is mediated by environmental paths alone. Heredity cannot mediate this association, because adoptive parents and their adopted children are not related genetically. In nonadoptive families, however, the association between I and P_c can be mediated, not only by environmental paths but also by a genetic chain of paths. (More on this later.) The point is that in addition to the direct environmental paths between the environmental measure and children's development, in nonadoptive families there is also an indirect association mediated by heredity.

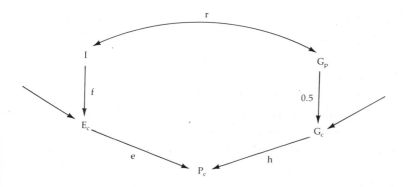

Figure 5.2. Path diagram illustrating the association between a measure of family environment and a measure of children's development in nonadoptive families in which parents and children share heredity as well as environment. (Adapted from Plomin, Loehlin & DeFries, 1985. Used with permission.)

As discussed in Box 3.6, path analysis permits us to visualize a model of the components (latent variables) underlying observed correlations. That is, the correlation between two variables in a particular model can be described as the product of the paths in the chain of paths from one variable to another. For example, the direct paths between the environmental index (I) and children's behavior (P_c) are fe, that is, the product of f and e. Suppose that for a particular environmental measure and a particular developmental measure, path f were 0.5 and path e were 0.4. This example would result in a phenotypic correlation of 0.20 (that is, 0.5×0.4) between the environmental measure and the measure of developmental outcome. In adoptive families, the model indicates that this is the only contributor to the correlation between the environmental measure and children's behavior. Thus, in our example, the actual correlation between the measures of environment and of development would be 0.20.

In nonadoptive families, in addition to this chain of environmental paths, there is an indirect chain of paths that goes through r, 0.5, and h (that is, 0.5rh). In path r (a simple correlation in this case, as depicted by the double-headed arrow) indicates that the environmental index (I) may be correlated with some unmeasured genetically influenced characteristics of the parent (G_p). For example, in the example of the association between the HOME and children's IQ, cognitive abilities of the parents or perhaps their sensitivity to their children's needs could be correlated genetically with the environmental index. The genetic chain of paths, 0.5rh, involves genetic effects via only one parent. Because both parents can contribute to the environment, the influence of both parents must be considered, and thus genetic mediation between the environmental index and children's IQ becomes 0.5rh + 0.5rh = rh.

In summary, the association between an environmental index and children's development in adoptive families is equivalent to fe. In nonadoptive families, the association can be represented by fe + rh. This discussion suggests a method to determine the extent of genetic involvement in environment-development associations: compare adoptive and nonadoptive families. If heredity is involved in relationships between measures of the home environment and children's development, environment-development correlations in nonadoptive families will be greater than in adoptive families. If heredity is not involved in the environment-development association, the correlation in nonadoptive families should be no greater than the correlation in adoptive families.

We can also estimate the extent to which an environment-development association is mediated genetically (rh) rather than environmentally (fe). The greater the differences between the correlations in the nonadoptive and adoptive families, the greater the extent to which the environment-development correlation is mediated genetically. The path model allows us to be more precise about this. The contributor to the association in adoptive families is fe. In nonadoptive families, contributions are made by fe but also by rh. Thus, the difference in correlations for nonadoptive and adoptive families is rh, the genetic component of the environment-development correlation.

In other words, given suitable data from adoptive families and comparable nonadoptive families, we can determine the extent to which the correlation between an environmental measure and a measure of children's development is due to genetic factors. The correlation in adoptive families directly estimates the environmental component. The difference between the correlations in nonadoptive families and adoptive families estimates the genetic component.

Adoption research on environment-development associations. Three earlier adoption studies that included measures of the home environment suggest substantial genetic mediation of the association between environmental measures and children's IQ, evidence that has gone unnoticed until recently. Across these three adoption studies, the average correlation between measures of the home environment and children's IQ is 0.45 in nonadoptive families and 0.18 in adoptive families. In the Colorado Adoption Project, similar results were found in infancy. For example, the HOME measure of the family environment correlated 0.44 with Bayley mental development scores at two years of age in nonadoptive homes. In adoptive homes, the correlation was 0.29. The HOME also correlates 0.50 with a measure of language development at two years in nonadoptive homes; in adoptive homes, the correlation was 0.32. Genetic mediation of environment-development associations is not limited to cognitive development: for example, genetic mediation was found between several measures involving familial "warmth" and measures of infant easy temperament (Plomin, Loehlin & DeFries, 1985).

In the Colorado Adoption Project, environment-development associations are generally weaker in early childhood than in infancy. Nonetheless, environment-development associations continue to be greater in nonadoptive homes than in adoptive homes. Moreover, longitudinal associations between environmental measures in infancy and developmental outcomes in childhood also show genetic mediation. For example, various environmental measures at 12 months of age correlate 0.42 with IQ at three years in nonadoptive families. In adoptive families, the correlation is 0.27 (Plomin, DeFries & Fulker, 1988).

Again, the most general implication of these results is that, in nonadoptive families, relationships between environmental measures and measures of development cannot be assumed to be environmental in origin. Behavioral genetic analyses indicate that it is safer to assume that fully half of environment-development associations is mediated genetically. One direction for future research is to identify parental and child characteristics that mediate genetic influence on associations between environmental measures and developmental outcomes. All we know so far is that the answer is not obvious. For example, it has been assumed that the relationship between the HOME measure of the family environment and mental development of children is freed from genetic influence when parental IQ is controlled—that is, when the effect of parental IQ is removed from the correlation between the HOME and children's mental development scores. However, analyses of data in the Colorado Adoption Project indicate that this is not the case. Even when parental IQ is statistically controlled, correlations between HOME scores and children's mental development scores continue to be substantially greater in nonadoptive than in adoptive families.

We are left with the intriguing implication that the parental characteristics responsible for genetic mediation of this association must be independent of parental IQ. Similar results are found for other domains of development: evidence for genetic mediation remains when traditional measures of parental cognitive ability and personality are controlled. In other words, genetic factors mediate associations between environmental measures and children's development. However, characteristics of parents through which this genetic mediation operates are not the characteristics of parents (such as cognitive ability and personality) we usually assess. Research aimed at understanding the factors responsible for genetic mediation of environment-development associations is likely to add enormously to our knowledge of significant features of parent-child interactions.

Summary

Other examples of the interface between nature and nurture include the topics of genotype-environment interaction and correlation, described briefly in Chapter 3. Behavioral genetic methods provide useful tools for studying these important issues as well. However, research has not yet made sufficient progress to warrant discussing these topics in this introduction to behavioral genetics. Nonetheless, the student of behavioral genetics must be aware that these other important issues exist at the interface between nature and nurture.

The three major topics of this chapter will suffice to make the case for the importance of behavioral genetics in studying nurture as well as nature: (1) behavioral genetics provides the best available evidence for the importance of environmental variance; (2) behavioral genetic research converges on the conclusion that environmental influences operate in ways quite different from what has been assumed—environmental variance relevant to behavioral development is primarily of the nonshared variety; and (3) behavioral genetic research indicates that heredity affects measures of the family environment as well as associations between environmental measures and measures of behavior.

The Future of Behavioral Genetics

This book has emphasized two messages. The first message is that genetic influence is important for many aspects of behavior, including cognitive abilities, personality, and psychopathology. Even within these major domains, we have just scratched the surface of possible applications of behavioral genetics. Little is known at all about other important dimensions of behavior, and these represent rich territory for future behavioral genetic exploration. Some possibilities include information processing and other experimental approaches to cognition, vulnerability and invulnerability to stress, emotional regulation, interests and attitudes, social cognition, familial and nonfamilial relationships, and life satisfaction.

In addition to these dimensions of behavior seen throughout the life span, behaviors important in the context of life
events and developmental transitions represent an outstanding
opportunity for future research. The possibilities are limitless,
including neonatal behavior, children's relationships with siblings and parents, the stresses of beginning school, the physical
and social transitions of early adolescence, entrance into the
adult world of work, marriage, childrearing behavior, and adjustment to the changes of later life.

The second message is just as important as the first: at
least as much variance in behavior is environmental as genetic.
During the 1970s and 1980s, the notion of genetic influence
on individual differences in behavior has become increasingly
appreciated. It is good that the social and behavioral sciences
have moved away from environmentalism. The danger now,
however, is that the rush from environmentalism will go too
far, to a view that all behavior is biologically determined.

During the 1970s, I found I had to speak gingerly about
genetic influence, gently suggesting that heredity might be important in behavior. Now, however, the transformation of the
social and behavioral sciences from environmentalism to
biological determinism is happening so fast that I find I more
often have to say, "Yes, genetic influences are substantial, but
environmental influences are important, too." I see this happening most clearly in the field of psychopathology, where the
search is on for single genes and simple neurochemical trig-
gers for schizophrenia, for example. Although it would be
splendid if some simple answer could be found for schizophrenia, this happy outcome seems highly unlikely for two
reasons. First, as indicated in Chapters 2 and 3, complex
behaviors, such as those diagnosed as schizophrenia, are likely
to be influenced by many genes, each with small effects. Second, schizophrenia is as much influenced by environmental
factors as it is by heredity. When we say that there is significant genetic influence on behavior, we often mean that genetic
influence is substantial, but we never mean total genetic deter-

mination. There are few complex behaviors for which more than half of the variance is explained by genetic differences among people. For cognitive abilities, psychopathology, and personality, most of the answer to the question of origins lies in nongenetic sources of influence.

As the pendulum of fashion swings from environmentalism to biological determinism, it is important that it be caught mid-swing, because behavioral genetic research clearly demonstrates that both nature and nurture are important in human development.

Resources

Nonshared Environment

A general resource concerning nonshared environment is a target article in the March 1987 issue of *Behavioral and Brain Sciences,* which is entitled "Why are children in the same family so different from one another?" (Plomin and Daniels, 10:1–16). This issue contains commentaries by 32 environmental and genetic researchers to the target article; the issue also contains a reply by the authors to these commentaries.

Nature and Nurture

Separate chapters in *Development, genetics, and psychology* by R. Plomin (Hillsdale, N.J.: Erlbaum, 1986) discuss in greater depth the issues of genetic influence on environmental measures and genetic mediation of environment-development associations.

References

Ahern, F. M., R. C. Johnson, J. R. Wilson, G. E. McClearn, and S. G. Vandenberg. 1982. Family resemblances in personality. *Behavior Genetics* 12:261-280

Anderson, V. E. 1974. Genetics and intelligence. In *Mental retardation and developmental disabilities: An annual review*, ed. J. Wortis. New York: Brunner/Mazel.

Bakwin, H. 1973. Reading disability in twins. *Developmental Medicine and Child Neurolgy* 15:184-187.

Baron, M., N. Risch, R. Hamburger, B. Mandel, and S. Kushner. 1987. Genetic linkage between X-chromosome markers and bipolar affective illness. *Nature* 326:289-292.

Bertelsen, A. 1979. A Danish twin study of manic-depressive disorders. In *Origin, prevention, and treatment of affective disorders*, eds. M. Schou & E. Stromgren. Orlando, Fla.: Academic Press.

Bertelsen, A. 1985. Controversies and consistencies in psychiatric genetics. *Acta Psychiatrica Scandinavica* 71:61-75.

Bertelsen, A., B. Harvald, and M. Hauge. 1977. A Danish twin study of manic-depressive disorders. *British Journal of Psychiatry* 130:330-351.

Bohman, M., C. R. Cloninger, A. -L. Knorring, and S. Sigvardsson. 1984. An adoption study of somatoform disorders III. Cross-fostering analysis and genetic relationship to alcoholism and criminality. *Archives of General Psychiatry* 41:872-878.

Bohman, M., S. Sigvardsson, and C. R. Cloninger. 1982. Maternal inheritance of alcohol abuse: Cross-fostering analysis of adopted women. *Archives of General Psychiatry* 38:965-969.

Bouchard, T. J., Jr. 1984. Twins reared together and apart: What they tell us about human diversity. In *Individuality and determinism*, ed. S. W. Fox. New York: Plenum.

Bouchard, T. J., Jr. 1987. Environmental determinants of IQ similarity in identical twins reared apart. Paper presented at the seventeenth annual meeting of the Behavior Genetics Association, Minneapolis, June 25.

Bouchard, T. J., Jr., and M. McGue. 1981. Familial studies of intelligence: A review. *Science* 212:1055-1059.

Buss, A. H., and R. Plomin. 1984. *Temperament: Early developing personality traits*. Hillsdale, N.J.: Erlbaum.

Caldwell, B. M., and R. H. Bradley. 1978. *Home observation for measurement of the environment*. Little Rock: University of Arkansas.

Canter, S. 1973. Personality traits in twins. In *Personality differences and biological variations*, eds. G. Claridge, S. Canter, and W. I. Hume. New York: Pergamon Press.

Carter, H. D. 1932. Twin similarities in occupational interests. *Journal of Educational Psychology* 23:641-655.

Christiansen, K. O. 1977. A preliminary study of criminality among twins. In *Biosocial bases of criminal behavior*, eds. S. A. Mednick and K. O. Christiansen. New York: Gardner.

Cloninger, C. R., M. Bohman, and S. Sigvardsson. 1981. Inheritance of alcohol abuse: Cross-fostering analysis of adopted men. *Archives of General Psychiatry* 38:861-869.

Cloninger, C. R., R. J. Martin, S. B. Guze, and P. J. Clayton. 1986. A prospective follow-up and family study of somatization in men and women. *American Journal of Psychiatry* 143:873–878.

Cotton, N. S. 1979. The familial incidence of alcoholism: A review. *Journal of Studies in Alcohol* 40:89–116.

Crowe, R. R., R. Noyes, D. L. Pauls, and D. Slymen. 1983. A family study of anxiety disorder. *Archives of General Psychiatry* 40:1065–1069.

Daniels, D. 1987. Differential experiences of siblings in the same family as predictors of adolescent sibling personality differences. *Journal of Personality and Social Psychology* 51:339–346.

Daniels, D., J. Dunn, F. F. Furstenberg, Jr., and R. Plomin. 1985. Environmental differences within the family and adjustment differences within pairs of adolescent siblings. *Child Development* 56:764–774.

Daniels, D., and R. Plomin. 1985. Differential experience of siblings in the same family. *Developmental Psychology* 21:747–760.

Decker, S. N., and S. G. Vandenberg. 1985. Colorado twin study of reading disability. In *Dyslexia: The study of the science*, eds. D. B. Gray and D. Pearl. New York: York.

DeFries, J. C. and D. W. Fulker. 1986. Multivariate behavioral genetics and development: An overview. *Behavior Genetics* 16:1–10.

DeFries, J. C., D. W. Fulker, and M. C. LaBuda. 1987. Evidence for a genetic etiology in reading disability in twins. *Nature* 329:537–539.

DeFries, J. C., M. C. Gervais, and E. A. Thomas. 1978. Response to 30 generations of selection for open-field activity in laboratory mice. *Behavior Genetics* 8:3–13.

DeFries, J. C., R. C. Johnson, A. R. Kuse, G. E. McClearn, J. Polovina, S. G. Vandenberg, and J. R. Wilson. 1979. Familial resemblance for specific cognitive abilities. *Behavior Genetics* 9:23–43.

DeFries, J. C. and R. Plomin. 1978. Behavioral genetics. *Annual Review of Psychology* 29:473–515.

DeFries, J. C., R. Plomin, and M. C. LaBuda. 1987. Genetic stability of cognitive development from childhood to adulthood. *Developmental Psychology* 23:4–12.

DeFries, J. C., S. G. Vandenberg, and G. E. McClearn. 1976. The genetics of specific cognitive abilities. *Annual Review of Genetics* 10:179–207.

DeFries, J. C., G. P. Vogler, and M. C. LaBuda. 1985. Colorado Family Reading Study: An overview. In *Behavior genetics: Principles and applications II*, eds. J. L. Fuller and E. C. Simmel. Hillsdale, N.J.: Erlbaum.

Detera-Wadleigh, S. D., W. H. Berrettini, L. R. Goldin, D. Boorman, S. Anderson, and E. S. Gershon. 1987. Close linkage of c-harvey-ras-1 and the insulin gene to affective disorder is ruled out in three North American pedigrees. *Nature* 325:806–808.

Dixon, L. K., and R. C. Johnson. 1980. *The roots of individuality: A survey of human behavior genetics*. Pacific Grove, Calif.: Brooks/Cole.

Dodson, E. O. 1956. *Genetics*. Philadelphia: Saunders.

Dunn, J. F., and R. Plomin. 1986. Determinants of maternal behavior toward three-year-old siblings. *British Journal of Developmental Psychology* 57:348–356.

Eaves, L. J., and P. A. Young. 1981. Genetical theory and personality differences. In *Dimensions of personality*, ed. R. Lynn. Oxford: Pergamon.

Egeland, J. A., D. S. Gerhard, D. L. Pauls, J. N. Sussex, and K. K. Kidd. 1987. Bipolar affective disorders linked to DNA markers on chromosome 11. *Nature* 325:783–787.

Ehrman, L., and P. A. Parsons. 1981. *The genetics of behavior*. Sunderland, Mass.: Sinauer Associates.

Erlenmeyer-Kimling, L., and B. Cornblatt. 1987. High-risk research in schizophrenia: A summary of what has been learned. *Journal of Psychiatric Research* 21:401–411.

Erlenmeyer-Kimling, L., and L. F. Jarvik. 1963. Genetics and intelligence: A review. *Science* 142:1477–1479.

Falconer, D. S. 1960. *Quantitative genetics*. New York: Ronald Press.

Falconer, D. S. 1965. The inheritance of liability to certain diseases. *Annals of Human Genetics* 29:51–76.

Falconer, D. S. 1981. *Introduction to quantitative genetics*. London: Longman.

Fisher, R. A. 1918. The correlation between relatives on the supposition of Mendelian inheritance. *Transactions of the Royal Society of Edinburgh* 52:399–433.

Floderus-Myrhed, B., N. L. Pedersen, and I. Rasmuson. 1980. Assessment of heritability for personality based on a short form of the Eysenck Personality Inventory: A study of 12,898 twin pairs. *Behavior Genetics* 10:153–162.

Folstein, S. and M. Rutter. 1977. Infantile autism: A genetic study of 21 twin pairs. *Journal of Child Psychology and Psychiatry* 18:297–332.

Fulker, D. W., R. Plomin, L. A. Thompson, K. Phillips, J. F. Fagan, III, and M. M. Haith. 1988. *Rapid screening of infant predictors of adult IQ: A study of twins and their parents.* Research report. University of Colorado, Boulder.

Fuller, J. L., and E. C. Simmel. 1983. *Behavior genetics: Principles and applications.* Hillsdale, N.J.: Erlbaum.

Fuller, J. L., and E. C. Simmel. 1985. *Behavior genetics: Principles and applications II.* Hillsdale, N.J.: Erlbaum.

Fuller, J. L., and W. R. Thompson. 1960. *Behavior genetics.* New York: Wiley.

Fuller, J. L., and W. R. Thompson. 1978. *Foundations of behavior genetics.* St. Louis: Mosby.

Galton, F. 1874. *English men of science: Their nature and nurture.* London: Macmillan.

Galton, F. 1875. The history of twins as a criterion of the relative powers of nature and nurture. *Journal of the Anthropological Institute* 6:391–406.

Gehring, W. J. 1987. Homeo boxes in the study of development. *Science* 236:1245–1252.

Gershon, E. S., J. L. Schreiber, J. R. Hamovit, E. D. Dibble, and W. Kaye. 1984. Clinical findings in patients with anorexia nervosa and affective illness in their relatives. *American Journal of Psychiatry* 141:1419–1422.

Gillberg, C., and J. Whalstrom. 1985. Chromosomal abnormalities in infantile autism and other childhood psychoses: A population study of 66 cases. *Developmental Medicine and Child Neurology* 27:293–304.

Goldgaber, D., M. I. Lerman, O. W. McBride, U. Saffiotti, and C. Gajdusek. 1987. Characterization and chromosomal localization of a DNA encoding brain amyloid of Alzheimer's disease. *Science* 235:877–880.

Goldsmith, H. H. 1983. Genetic influence on personality from infancy to adulthood. *Child Development* 54:331–355.

Goldsmith, H. H., and J. J. Campos. 1986. Fundamental issues in the study of early temperament: The Denver Twin Temperament Study. In *Advances in developmental psychology,* eds. M. E. Lamb, A. L. Brown, and B. Rogoff. Hillsdale, N.J.: Erlbaum.

Goodwin, D. W. 1976. *Is alcoholism hereditary?* New York: Oxford University.

Gottesman, I. I., G. Carey, and D. R. Hanson. 1983. Pearls and perils in epigenetic psychopathology. In *Childhood psychopathology and development,* eds. S. B. Guze, E. J. Earls, and J. E. Barrett. New York: Raven Press.

Gottesman, I. I., and J. Shields. 1982. *Schizophrenia: The epigenetic puzzle.* Cambridge: Cambridge University Press.

Guilford, J. P., and B. Fruchter. 1973. *Fundamental statistics in psychology and education.* New York: McGraw-Hill.

Gusella, J. F., N. S. Wexler, P. M. Conneally, S. L. Naylor, M. A. Anderson, R. E. Tanzi, P. C. Watkins, and K. Ottina. 1983. A polymorphic DNA marker genetically linked to Huntington's disease. *Nature* 306:234–238.

Guze, S. B., C. R. Cloninger, R. L. Martin, and P. J. Clayton. 1986. A follow-up and family study of Briquet's syndrome. *British Journal of Psychiatry* 149:17–23.

Hay, D. A. 1985. *Essentials of behaviour genetics.* Oxford: Blackwells.

Henderson, N. D. 1982. Human behavior genetics. *Annual Review of Psychology* 33:403–440.

Heston, L. L. 1966. Psychiatric disorders in foster home reared children of schizophrenic mothers. *British Journal of Psychiatry* 112:819–825.

Heston, L. L., and A. R. Mastri. 1977. The genetics of Alzheimer's disease: Associations with hematologic malignancy and Down's syndrome. *Archives of General Psychiatry* 34:976–981.

Hodgkinson, S., R. Sherrington, H. Gurling,

R. Marchbanks, and S. Reeders. 1987. Molecular genetic evidence for heterogeneity in manic depression. *Nature* 325:805–806.

Holland, A. J., A. Hall, R. Murray, G. F. M. Russell, and A. H. Crisp. 1984. Anorexia nervosa: A study of 34 twin pairs and one set of triplets. *British Journal of Psychiatry* 145:414–419.

Holm, N. V., M. Hauge, and O. M. Jensen. 1982. Studies of cancer aetiology in a complete twin population: Breast cancer, colorectal cancer and leukaemia. *Cancer Surveys* 1:17–32.

Hrubec, Z., and G. S. Omenn. 1981. Evidence of genetic predisposition to alcohol cirrhosis and psychosis: Twin concordances for alcoholism and its biological end points by zygosity among male veterans. *Alcoholism: Clinical and Experimental Research* 5:207–215.

Husén, T. 1959. *Psychological twin research: A methodological study.* Stockholm: Almqvist & Wiksell.

Jensen, A. R. 1969. How much can we boost IQ and scholastic achievement? *Harvard Educational Review* 39:1–123.

Jensen, A. R. 1980. *Bias in mental testing.* New York: Free Press.

Jinks, J. L., and D. W. Fulker. 1970. Comparison of the biometrical genetical, MAVA, and classical approaches to the analysis of human behavior. *Psychological Bulletin* 73:311–349.

Johnson, C. A., F. M. Ahern, and R. C. Johnson. 1976. Level of functioning of siblings and parents of probands of varying degrees of retardation. *Behavior Genetics* 6:473–477.

Judson, H. F. 1986. *The eighth day of creation: Makers of the revolution in biology.* New York: Simon & Schuster.

Kallmann, F. J. 1955. Genetic aspects of mental disorders in later life. In *Mental disorders in later life,* ed. O. J. Kaplan. Stanford, Calif.: Stanford University Press.

Kendler, K. S., and C. D. Robinette. 1983. Schizophrenia in the National Academy of Sciences-National Research Council twin registry: A 16-year update. *American Journal of Psychiatry* 140:1551–1563.

Kennedy, J. L., L. A. Giuffra, H. W. Moises, L. L. Cavalli-Sforza, A. J. Pakstis, J. R. Kidd,

C. M. Castiglione, B. Sjogren, L. Wetterberg, and K. K. Kidd. 1988. Evidence against linkage of schizophrenia to markers on chromosome 5 in a northern Swedish pedigree. *Nature* 336: 167–170.

Kety, S. S., D. Rosenthal, P. H. Wender, and F. Schulsinger. 1976. Studies based on a total sample of adopted individuals and their relatives: Why they were necessary, what they demonstrated and failed to demonstrate. *Schizophrenia Bulletin* 2:413–428.

Kimberling, W. J., P. R. Fain, P. S. Ing, S. D. Smith, and B. F. Pennington. 1985. Linkage analysis of reading disability with chromosome 15. *Behavior Genetics* 15:597–598.

LaBuda, M., J. C. DeFries, and D. W. Fulker. 1987. Genetic and environmental covariance structures among WISC-R subtests: A twin study. *Intelligence* 11:233–244.

Lerner, I. M., and W. J. Libby. 1976. *Heredity, evolution and society.* San Francisco: W. H. Freeman.

Loehlin, J. C. 1982. Are personality traits differentially heritable? *Behavior Genetics* 12:417–428.

Loehlin, J. C. 1987. *Latent variable models.* Hillsdale, N.J.: Erlbaum.

Loehlin, J. C., and R. C. Nichols. 1976. *Heredity, environment, and personality.* Austin: University of Texas Press.

Loehlin, J. C., L. Willerman, and J. M. Horn. 1988. Human behavior genetics. *Annual Review of Psychology* 39:101–133.

Ludlow, C. L. and J. A. Cooper. 1983. *Genetic aspects of speech and language disorders.* New York: Academic Press.

McGuffin, P. 1987. The new genetics and childhood psychiatric disorder. *Journal of Child Psychology and Psychiatry* 28:215–222.

McKusick, V. A. 1989. *Mendelian inheritance in man.* 9th ed. Baltimore: Johns Hopkins University Press.

Martin, N. G., L. J. Eaves, A. C. Heath, R. Jardine, L. M. Feingold, and H. J. Eysenck. 1986. Transmission of social attitudes. *Proceedings of the National Academy of Sciences, USA* 83:4364–4368.

Martin, N. G., and R. Jardine. 1986. Eysenck's contributions to behavior genetics. In *Hans Eysenck: Consensus and contro-*

versy, eds. S. Modgil and C. Modgil. Philadelphia: Falmer.

Mednick, S. A., W. F. Gabrielli, Jr., and B. Hutchings. 1984. Genetic influences in criminal convictions: Evidence from an adoption cohort. *Science* 224:891–894.

Mednick, S. A., T. E. Moffitt, and S. Stack. 1987. *The causes of crime: New biological approaches.* New York: Cambridge University Press.

Mendel, G. J. 1866. Versuche über pflanzenhybriden. (Experiments in plant hybridization.) *Verhandlungen des Naturforschunden Vereines in Bruenn* 4:3–47.

Murphey, R. M. 1983. Phenylketonuria (PKU) and the single gene: An old story retold. *Behavior Genetics* 13:141–157.

Nathan, M., and R. Guttman. 1984. Similarities in test scores and profiles of kibbutz twins and singletons. *Acta Geneticae Medicae Gemellologiae* 33:213–218.

Nee, L. E., R. Eldridge, T. Sunderland, C. B. Thomas, and D. Katz. 1987. Dementia of the Alzheimer type: Clinical and family study of 22 twin pairs. *Neurology* 37:259–363.

Nichols, P. L. 1984. Familial mental retardation. *Behavior Genetics* 14:161–170.

Nichols, R. C. 1978. Twin studies of ability, personality, and interests. *Homo* 29:158–173.

Nurnberger, J. I., and E. S. Gershon. 1981. Genetics of affective disorders. In *Depression and antidepressants: Implications for courses and treatment*, ed. E. Friedman. New York: Raven.

Nussbaum, R. L., and D. H. Ledbetter. 1986. Fragile X syndrome: A unique mutation in man. *Annual Review of Genetics* 20:109–145.

Oliverio, A. 1977. *Genetics, environment, and intelligence.* Amsterdam: Elsevier.

Orvaschel, H. 1983. Maternal depression and child dysfunction: Children at risk. In *Advances in clinical child psychology*, eds. B. B. Lahey and A. E. Kazdin. New York: Plenum.

Pedersen, N. L., L. Friberg, B. Floderus-Myrhed, G. E. McClearn, and R. Plomin. 1984. Swedish early separated twins: Identification and characterization. *Acta Geneticae Medicae et Gemellologiae* 33:243–250.

Pedersen, N. L., R. Plomin, G. E. McClearn, and L. Friberg. 1988. Neuroticism, extraversion and related traits in adult twins reared apart and reared together. *Journal of Personality and Social Psychology* 55, 950–957.

Peele, S. 1986. The implications and limitations of genetic models of alcoholism and other addictions. *Journal of Studies on Alcohol* 47:63–73.

Pennington, B. F., and S. D. Smith. 1983. Genetic influences on learning disabilities and speech and language disorders. *Child Development* 54:369–387.

Plomin, R. 1981. Heredity and temperament: A comparison of twin data for self-report questionnaires, parental ratings, and objectively assessed behavior. In *Twin research 3: Intelligence, personality, and development*, eds. L. Gedda, P. Parisi, and W. E. Nance. New York: Liss.

Plomin, R. 1986. *Development, genetics, and psychology.* Hillsdale, N.J.: Erlbaum.

Plomin, R. 1988. The nature and nurture of cognitive abilities. In *Advances in the psychology of human intelligence*, ed. R. J. Sternberg. Hillsdale, N.J.: Erlbaum.

Plomin, R., and D. Daniels. 1987. Why are children in the same family so different from each other? *Behavioral and Brain Sciences* 10:1–16.

Plomin, R., and J. C. DeFries. 1980. Genetics and intelligence: Recent data. *Intelligence* 4:15–24.

Plomin, R., and J. C. DeFries. 1985. *Origins of individual differences in infancy: The Colorado Adoption Project.* New York: Academic Press.

Plomin, R., J. C. DeFries, and D. W. Fulker. 1988. *Nature and nurture during infancy and early childhood.* New York: Cambridge University Press.

Plomin, R., J. C. DeFries, and J. C. Loehlin. 1977. Genotype-environment interaction and correlation in the analysis of human behavior. *Psychological Bulletin* 84:309–322.

Plomin, R., J. C. DeFries, and G. E. McClearn. 1989. *Behavioral genetics: A primer.* 2nd ed. New York: W. H. Freeman.

Plomin, R., T. T. Foch, and D. C. Rowe. 1981. Bobo clown aggression in childhood: Environment, not genes. *Journal of Research in Personality* 15:331–342.

Plomin, R., and J. C. Loehlin. In press. Direct and indirect heritability estimates. *Behavior Genetics.*

Plomin, R., J. C. Loehlin, and J. C. DeFries. 1985. Genetic and environmental components of "environmental" influences. *Developmental Psychology* 21: 391–402.

Plomin, R., G. E. McClearn, N. L. Pedersen, J. R. Nesselroade, and C. S. Bergeman. 1988. Genetic influence on childhood family environment perceived retrospectively from the last half of the life span. *Developmental Psychology* 24:738–745.

Plomin, R., N. L. Pedersen, G. E. McClearn, J. R. Nesselroade, and C. S. Bergeman. 1988. EAS temperaments during the last half of the life span: Twins reared apart and twins reared together. *Psychology and Aging* 3:43–50.

Plomin, R., and D. C. Rowe. 1979. Genetic and environmental etiology of social behavior in infancy. *Developmental Psychology* 15:62–72.

Reed, E. W., and S. C. Reed. 1965. *Mental retardation: A family study.* Philadelphia: Saunders.

Reich, T., P. Van Eerdewegh, J. Rice, J. Mullaney, J. Endicott, and G. L. Klerman. 1987. The familial transmission of primary major depressive disorder. *Journal of Psychiatric Research* 21:613–624.

Renvoize, E. B., R. H. S. Mindham, M. Stewart, R. McDonald, and D. R. D. Wallace. 1986. Identical twins discordant for presenile dementia of the Alzheimer type. *British Journal of Psychiatry* 149:509–512.

Reznikoff, M., G. Domino, C. Bridges, and M. Honeyman. 1973. Creative abilities in identical and fraternal twins. *Behavior Genetics* 3:365–377.

Rice, J. P., T. Reich, N. C. Andreasen, J. Endicott, M. Van Eerdewegh, A. Fishman, R. M. A. Hirschfield, and G. L. Klerman. 1987. The familial transmission of bipolar illnesses. *Archives of General Psychiatry* 41:441–447.

Ritvo, E. R., B. J. Freeman, A. Mason-Brothers, A. Mo, and A. M. Ritvo. 1985. Concordance for the syndrome of autism in 40 pairs of affected twins. *American Journal of Psychiatry* 142:74–77.

Roberts, C. A., and C. B. Johansson. 1974. The inheritance of cognitive interest styles among twins. *Journal of Vocational Behavior* 4:237–243.

Robins, L. N., J. E. Helzer, M. M. Weissmann, H. Orvaschel, E. Gruenberg, J. D. Burke, and D. A. Regier. 1984. Lifetime prevalence of specific psychiatric disorders in three sites. *Archives of General Psychiatry* 41:949–958.

Rosenthal, D. 1970. *Genetic theory and abnormal behavior.* New York: McGraw-Hill.

Rosenthal, D. 1972. Three adoption studies of heredity in the schizophrenic disorders. *International Journal of Mental Health* 1:63–75.

Rowe, D. C. 1981. Environmental and genetic influences on dimensions of perceived parenting: A twin study. *Developmental Psychology* 17:203–208.

Rowe, D. C. 1983a. A biometrical analysis of perceptions of family environment: A study of twin and singleton sibling kinships. *Child Development* 54:416–423.

Rowe, D. C. 1983b. Biometrical genetic models of self-reported delinquent behavior: Twin study. *Behavior Genetics* 13:473–489.

Scarr, S., and R. A. Weinberg. 1978a. Attitudes, interests, and IQ. *Human Nature* (April):29–36.

Scarr, S., and R. A. Weinberg. 1978b. The influence of "family background" on intellectual attainment. *American Sociological Review* 43:674–692.

Schellenberg, G. D., T. D. Bird, E. M. Wijsman, D. K. Moore, M. Boehnke, E. M. Bryant, T. H. Lampe, D. Nochlin, S. M. Sumi, S. S. Deeb, K. Beyreuther, and G. M. Martin. 1988. Absence of linkage of chromosome 21q21 markers to familial Alzheimer's disease. *Science* 241:1507–1510.

Segal, N. 1986. Monozygotic and dizygotic twins: A comparative analysis of mental ability profiles. *Child Development* 56:1051–1058.

Sherrington, R., J. Brynjolfsson, H. Petursson, M. Potter, K. Dudleston, B. Barraclough, J. Wasmuth, M. Dobbs, and H. Gurling. 1988. Localization of a susceptibility locus for schizophrenia on chromosome 5. *Nature* 336:164–167.

Sigvardsson, S., C. R. Cloninger, and M. Bohman. 1985. Prevention and treatment of alcohol abuse: Uses and limitations of the high risk paradigm. *Social Biology* 32:185–194.

Smith, S. D., W. J. Kimberling, B. F. Pennington, and H. A. Lubs. 1983. Specific reading disability: Identification of an inherited form through linkage analysis. *Science* 219:1345–1347.

Snyderman, M., and S. Rothman. 1987. Survey of expert opinion on intelligence and aptitude testing. *American Psychologist* 42:137–144.

Stevenson, J., P. Graham, G. Fredman, and V. McLoughlin. 1987. A twin study of genetic influences on reading and spelling ability and disability. *Journal of Child Psychology and Psychiatry* 28:229–247.

Tambs, K., J. M. Sundet, and P. Magnus. 1984. Heritability analysis of the WAIS subtests: A study of twins. *Intelligence* 8:283–293.

Tellegen, A., D. T. Lykken, T. J. Bouchard, K. Wilcox, N. L. Segal, and S. Rich. 1988. Personality similarity in twins reared apart and together. *Journal of Social and Personality Psychology* 54:1031–1039.

Terman, L. M. and M. A. Merrill. 1973. *Stanford-Binet intelligence scale: 1972 norms edition.* Boston: Houghton-Mifflin.

Tryon, R. C. 1942. Individual differences. In *Comparative psychology,* ed. F. A. Moss. Englewood Cliffs, N.J.: Prentice-Hall.

Tsuang, M. T., and R. Vandermey. 1980. *Genes and the mind: Inheritance of mental illness.* Oxford: Oxford University Press.

Vandenberg, S. G., S. M. Singer, and D. L. Pauls. 1986. *The heredity of behavioral disorders in adults and children.* New York: Plenum.

Vernon, P. E. 1979. *Intelligence: Heredity and environment.* San Francisco: W. H. Freeman.

Watson, J. B. 1925. *Behaviorism.* London: Kegan Paul, Trench, Trubner.

Watson, J. D. 1968. *The double helix.* New York: Atheneum.

Watson, J. D., and J. Tooze. 1981. *The DNA story.* San Francisco: W. H. Freeman.

Watson, J. D., J. Tooze, and D. T. Kurtz. 1983. *Recombinant DNA: A short course.* New York: Scientific American Books.

Watt, N. F., E. J. Anthony, L. C. Wynne, and J. E. Rolf. 1984. *Children at risk for schizophrenia: A longitudinal perspective.* Cambridge: Cambridge University Press.

Wender, P. H., S. S. Kety, D. Rosenthal, F. Schulsinger, J. Ortmann, and I. Lunde. 1986. Psychiatric disorders in the biological and adoptive families of adopted individuals with affective disorders. *Archives of General Psychiatry* 43:923–939.

Wilson, J. Q., and R. J. Herrnstein. 1985. *Crime and human nature.* New York: Simon & Schuster.

Wilson, R. S. 1975. Twins: Patterns of cognitive development as measured on the WPPSI. *Developmental Psychology* 11:126–139.

Wilson, R. S., and A. P. Matheny, Jr. 1986. Behavior-genetics research in infant temperament: The Louisville Twin Study. In *The study of temperament: Changes, continuities and challenges,* eds. R. Plomin and J. Dunn. Hillsdale, N.J.: Erlbaum.

Wright, S. 1921. Correlation and causation. *Journal of Agricultural Research* 20:557–585.

Author Index

Subject Index